HELPING *angry* PEOPLE

Other books in the Strategic Pastoral Counseling Resources series

HELPING

angry

PEOPLE

GLENN TAYLOR
AND ROD WILSON

STRATEGIC PASTORAL COUNSELING RESOURCES

BakerBooks

A Division of Baker Book House Co
Grand Rapids, Michigan 49516

©1997 by Glenn Taylor and Rod Wilson

Published by Baker Books
a division of Baker Book House Company
P.O. Box 6287, Grand Rapids, MI 49516-6287

Printed in the United States of America

ISBN 0-8010-9043-1

Library of Congress Cataloging-in-Publication Data is on file at the Library of Congress, Washington, D.C.

For information about academic books, resources for Christian leaders, and all new releases available from Baker Book House, visit our web site:
http://www.bakerbooks.com

To our wives, Bev Wilson and Mary Taylor,
who along with our children have provided a context
of support and acceptance for exploring human relationships
including the understanding and expression of anger.

CONTENTS

SERIES PREFACE

AN INTRODUCTION TO STRATEGIC PASTORAL COUNSELING

DAVID G. BENNER

While the provision of spiritual counsel has been an integral part of Christian soul care since the earliest days of the church, the contemporary understanding and practice of pastoral counseling is largely a product of the twentieth century. Developing within the shadow of the modern psychotherapies, pastoral counseling has derived much of its style and approach from these clinical therapeutics. What this has meant is that pastoral counselors have often seen themselves more as counselors than as pastors and the counseling that they have provided has often been a rather awkward adaptation of clinical counseling models to a pastoral context. This, in turn, has often resulted in significant tension between the pastoral and psychological dimensions of the counseling provided by clergy and others in Christian ministry. It is also frequently reflected in pastoral counselors who are more interested in anything connected with the modern mystery cult of psychotherapy than with their own tradition of Christian soul care, and who, as a consequence, are often quite insecure in their pastoral role and identity.

While pastoral counseling owes much to the psychological culture that has gained ascendancy in the West during the past century, this influence has quite clearly been a mixed blessing. Contemporary pastoral counselors typically offer their help with much
more psychological sophistication than was the case several
decades ago, but all too often they do so without a clear sense of
the uniqueness of counseling that is offered by a pastor. And not
only are the distinctive spiritual resources of Christian ministry
often deemphasized or ignored, but the tensions that are associated with attempts to directly translate clinical models of counseling into the pastoral context become a source of much frustration. This is in part why so many pastors report dissatisfaction
with their counseling. While they indicate that this dissatisfaction
is a result of insufficient training in and time for counseling, a big-
ger part of the problem may be that pastors have been offered
approaches to counseling that are of questionable appropriateness for the pastoral context and that will inevitably leave them
feeling frustrated and inadequate.

Strategic Pastoral Counseling is a model of counseling that has
been specifically designed to fit the role, resources, and needs of
the typical pastor who counsels. Information about this "typical"
pastor was solicited by means of a survey of over 400 pastors (this
research is described in the introductory volume of the series,
Strategic Pastoral Counseling: A Short-Term Structured Model [Benner,
1992]). The model appropriates the insights of contemporary
counseling theory without sacrificing the resources of pastoral
ministry. Furthermore, it takes its form and direction from the
pastoral role and in so doing offers an approach to counseling that
is not only congruent with the other aspects of pastoral ministry
but that places pastoral counseling at the very heart of ministry.

The present volume represents an application of Strategic Pastoral Counseling to one commonly encountered problem situation. As such, it presupposes a familiarity with the basic model.
Readers not familiar with *Strategic Pastoral Counseling: A Short-Term
Structured Model* should consult that book for a detailed presentation of the model and its implementation. What follows is a brief
review of this material which, while it does not adequately summarize all that is presented in that book, should serve as a reminder

of the most important features of the Strategic Pastoral Counseling approach.

The Strategic Pastoral Counseling Model

Strategic Pastoral Counseling is short-term, bibliotherapeutic, wholistic, structured, spiritually focused, and explicitly Christian. Each of these characteristics will be briefly discussed in order.

Short-Term Counseling

Counseling can be brief (that is, conducted over a relatively few sessions), time-limited (that is, conducted within an initially fixed number of total sessions), or both. Strategic Pastoral Counseling is both brief and time-limited, working within a suggested maximum of five sessions. The decision to set this upper limit on the number of sessions was in response to the fact that the background research conducted in the design of the model indicated that 87 percent of the pastoral counseling conducted by pastors in general ministry involves five sessions or less. This short-term approach to counseling seems ideally suited to the time availability, training, and role demands of pastors.

Recent research in short-term counseling has made it clear that while such an approach requires that the counselor be diligent in maintaining the focus on the single agreed upon central problem, significant and enduring changes can occur through a very small number of counseling sessions. Strategic Pastoral Counseling differs, in this regard, from the more ongoing relationship of discipleship or spiritual guidance. In these, the goal is the development of spiritual maturity. Strategic Pastoral Counseling has a much more modest goal: examining a particular problem or experience in the light of God's will for and activity in the life of the individual seeking help and attempting to facilitate growth in and through that person's present life situation. While this is still an ambitious goal, its focused nature makes it quite attainable within a short period of time. It is this focus that makes the counseling strategic.

The five-session limit should be communicated by the pastor no later than the first session and preferably in the prior conversation when the time is set for this session. This ensures that the parishioner is aware of the time limit from the beginning and can share responsibility in keeping the counseling sessions focused. Some people will undoubtedly require more than five sessions in order to bring about a resolution of their problems. These people should be referred to someone who is appropriately qualified for such work; preparation for this referral will be one of the goals of the five sessions. However, the fact that such people may require more help than can be provided in five sessions of pastoral counseling does not mean that they cannot benefit from such focused short-term pastoral care; no individuals should be regarded as inappropriate candidates for Strategic Pastoral Counseling merely because they may require other help.

One final but important note about the suggested limit of five sessions is that this does not have to be tied to a corresponding period of five weeks. In fact, many pastors find weekly sessions to be less useful than sessions scheduled two or three weeks apart. This sort of spacing of the last couple of sessions is particularly helpful and should be considered even if the first several sessions are held weekly.

Bibliotherapeutic Counseling

Bibliotherapy refers to the therapeutic use of reading. Strategic Pastoral Counseling builds the use of written materials into the heart of its approach to pastoral caregiving. The Bible itself is, of course, a rich bibliotherapeutic resource and the encouragement of and direction in its reading is an important part of Strategic Pastoral Counseling. Its use must be disciplined and selective and particular care must be taken to ensure that it is never employed in a mechanical or impersonal manner. However, when used appropriately it can unquestionably be one of the most dynamic and powerful resources available to the pastor who counsels.

While the Bible is a unique bibliotherapeutic resource, it is not the only such resource. Strategic Pastoral Counseling comes with a built-in set of specifically designed resources. Each of the 10 volumes in this series has an accompanying book written for the parishioner who is being seen in counseling. These resource books are written by the same authors as the volumes for pastors and are designed for easy integration into counseling sessions.

The use of reading materials that are consistent with the counseling being provided can serve as a most significant support and extension of the counseling offered by a pastor. The parishioner now has a helping resource that is not limited by the pastor's time and availability. Furthermore, the pastor can now allow the written materials to do part of the work of counseling, using the sessions to deal with those matters that are not as well addressed through the written page.

Wholistic Counseling

It might seem surprising to suggest that a short-term counseling approach should also be wholistic. But this is both possible and highly desirable. Wholistic counseling is counseling that is responsive to the totality of the complex psycho-spiritual dynamics that make up the life of human persons. Biblical psychology is clearly a wholistic psychology. The various "parts" of persons (i.e., body, soul, spirit, heart, flesh, etc.) are never presented as separate faculties or independent components of persons but always as different ways of seeing the whole person. Biblical discussions of persons emphasize first and foremost their essential unity of being. Humans are ultimately understandable only in the light of this primary and irreducible wholeness, and helping efforts that are truly Christian must resist the temptation to see persons only through their thoughts, feelings, behaviors, or any other single manifestation of being.

The alternative to wholism in counseling is to focus on only one of these modalities of functioning and this is, indeed, what many approaches to counseling do. In contrast, Strategic Pastoral Counseling asserts that pastoral counseling must be responsive to the behavioral (action), cognitive (thought), and affective (feeling) elements of personal functioning. Each examined separately can obscure that which is really going on with a person. But taken together they form the basis for a comprehensive assessment and effective intervention. Strategic Pastoral Counseling provides a framework for ensuring that each of these spheres of functioning is addressed and this, in fact, provides much of the structure for the counseling.

Structured Counseling

The structured nature of Strategic Pastoral Counseling is that which enables its brevity, ensuring that each of the sessions has a clear focus and that each builds upon the previous ones in contributing to the accomplishment of the overall goals. The framework that structures Strategic Pastoral Counseling is sufficiently tight as to enable the pastor to provide a wholistic assessment and counseling intervention within a maximum of five sessions and yet it is also sufficiently flexible to allow for differences in individual styles of different counselors. This is very important because Strategic Pastoral Counseling is not primarily a set of techniques but an intimate encounter of and dialogue between people.

The structure of Strategic Pastoral Counseling grows out of the goal of addressing the feelings, thoughts, and behaviors that are part of the troubling experiences of the person seeking help. It is also a structure that is responsive to the several tasks that face the pastoral counselor, tasks such as conducting an initial assessment, developing a general understanding of the problem and of the person's major needs, and selecting and delivering interventions and resources that will bring help. This structure is described in more detail later.

Spiritually Focused Counseling

The fifth distinctive of Strategic Pastoral Counseling is that it is spiritually focused. This does not mean that only religious matters are discussed. Our spirituality is our essential heart commitments, our basic life direction, and our fundamental allegiances. These spiritual aspects of our being are, of course, reflected in our attitudes toward God and are expressed in our explicitly religious values and behaviors. However, they are also reflected in matters that may seem on the surface to be much less religious. Strategic Pastoral Counselors place a primacy on listening to this underlying spiritual story. They listen for what we might call the story behind the story.

But listening to the story behind the story requires that one first listen to and take seriously the presenting story. To disregard the presenting situation is spiritualization of a problem. It fails to take the problem seriously and makes a mockery of counseling as genuine dialogue. The Strategic Pastoral Counselor thus listens to and enters into the experience of parishioners as they relate their struggles and life's experiences. But while this is a real part of the story, it is not the whole story that must be heard and understood. For in the midst of this story emerges another: the story of the spiritual response to these experiences. This response may be one of unwavering trust in God but a failure to expect much of him. Or it may be one of doubt, anger, confusion, or despair. Each of these is a spiritual response to present struggles and in one form or another, the spiritual aspect of the person's experience will always be discernible to the pastor who watches for it. Strategic Pastoral Counseling makes this underlying spiritual story the primary focus.

Explicitly Christian Counseling

While it is important to not confuse spirituality with religiosity, it is equally important to not confuse Christian spirituality with any of its imitations. In this regard, it is crucial that Strategic Pastoral Counseling be distinctively and explicitly Christian. And while Strategic Pastoral Counseling begins with a focus on spiritual matters understood broadly, its master goal is to facilitate the other person's awareness of and response to the call of God to surrender and service. This is the essential and most important distinctive of Strategic Pastoral Counseling.

One of the ways in which Strategic Pastoral Counseling is made explicitly Christian is through its utilization of Christian theological language, images, and concepts and the religious resources of prayer, Scripture, and the sacraments. These resources must never be used in a mechanical, legalistic, or magical fashion. But used sensitively and wisely, they can be the conduit for a dynamic contact between God and the person seeking pastoral help. And this is the goal of their utilization, not some superficial baptizing of the counseling in order to make it Christian but rather a way of bringing the one seeking help more closely in touch with the God who is the source of all life, growth, and healing.

Another important resource that is appropriated by the Strategic Pastoral Counselor is that of the church as a community. Too often pastoral counseling is conducted in a way that is not appreciably different from that which might be offered by a Christian counselor in private practice. This most unfortunate practice ignores the rich resources that are potentially available in any Christian congregation. One of the most important ways in which Strategic Pastoral Counseling is able to maintain its short-term nature is by the pastor connecting the person seeking help with others in the church who can provide portions of that help. The congregation can, of course, also be involved in less individualistic ways. Support and ministry groups of various sorts are becoming a part of many congregations that seek to provide a dynamic ministry to their community and are potentially important resources for the Strategic Pastoral Counselor.

A final and even more fundamental way in which Strategic Pastoral Counseling is Christian is in the reliance that it encourages on the Holy Spirit. The Spirit is the indispensable source of all wisdom that is necessary for the practice of pastoral counseling. Recognizing that all healing and growth are ultimately of God, the Strategic Pastoral Counselor can thus take comfort in this reliance on the Spirit of God and on the fact that ultimate responsibility for people and their well-being lies with God.

Stages and Tasks of Strategic Pastoral Counseling

The three overall stages that organize Strategic Pastoral Counseling can be described as *encounter, engagement,* and *disengagement.* The first stage of Strategic Pastoral Counseling, encounter, corresponds to the initial session in which the goal is to establish personal contact with the person seeking help, set the boundaries for the counseling relationship, become acquainted with that person and the central concerns, conduct a pastoral diagnosis, and develop a mutually acceptable focus for the subsequent sessions. The second stage, engagement, involves the pastor moving beyond the first contact and establishing a deeper working alliance with the person seeking help. This normally occupies the next one to three sessions and entails the exploration of the person's feelings, thoughts, and behavioral patterns associated with this problem area and the development of new perspectives and strategies for coping or change. The third and final stage, disengagement, describes the focus of the last one or possibly two sessions, and involves an evaluation of progress and an assessment of remaining concerns, the making of a referral for further help if this is needed, and the ending of the counseling relationship. These stages and tasks are summarized in the table below.

Stages and Tasks of Strategic Pastoral Counseling

Stage 1: Encounter (Session 1)
- Joining and boundary-setting
- Exploring the central concerns and relevant history
- Conducting a pastoral diagnosis
- Achieving a mutually agreeable focus for counseling

Stage 2: Engagement (Sessions 2, 3, 4)
- Exploration of cognitive, affective, and behavioral aspects of the problem and the identification of resources for coping or change

Stage 3: Disengagement (Sessions 4, 5)
- Evaluation of progress and assessment of remaining concerns
- Referral (if needed)
- Termination of counseling

The Encounter Stage

The first task in this initial stage of Strategic Pastoral Counseling is joining and boundary-setting. Joining involves putting the parishioner at ease by means of a few moments of casual conversation that is designed to ease pastor and parishioner into contact. Such preliminary conversation should never take more than five minutes and should usually be kept to two or three. It will not always be necessary, because some people are immediately ready to tell their story. Boundary-setting involves the communication of the purpose of this session and the time frame for the session and your work together. This should not normally require more than a sentence or two.

The exploration of central concerns and relevant history usually begins with an invitation for parishioners to describe what led them to seek help at the present time. After hearing an expression of these immediate concerns, it is usually helpful to get a brief historical perspective on these concerns and the person. Ten to 15 minutes of exploration of the course of development of the presenting problems and their efforts to cope or get help with them is the foundation of this part of the session. It is also important at this point to get some idea of the parishioner's present living and family arrangements as well as work and/or educational situation. The organizing thread for this section of the first interview should be the presenting problem. These matters will not be the only ones discussed but this focus serves to give the session the necessary direction.

Stripped of its distracting medical connotations, diagnosis is problem definition and this is a fundamental part of any approach to counseling. Diagnoses involve judgments about the nature of the problem and, either implicitly or explicitly, pastoral counselors make such judgments every time they commence a counseling relationship. But in order for diagnoses to be relevant they must guide the counseling that will follow. This means that the categories of pastoral assessment must be primarily related to the spiritual focus, which is foundational to any counseling that is appropriately called pastoral. Thus, the diagnosis called for in the first stage of Strategic Pastoral Counseling involves an assessment of the person's spiritual well-being.

The framework for pastoral diagnosis adopted by Strategic Pastoral Counseling is that suggested by Malony (1988) and used as the basis of his Religious Status Interview. Malony proposed that the diagnosis of Christian religious well-being should involve the assessment of the person's awareness of God, acceptance of God's grace, repentance and responsibility, response to God's leadership and direction, involvement in the church, experience of fellowship, ethics, and openness in the faith. While this approach to pastoral diagnosis has been found to be helpful by many, the Strategic Pastoral Counselor need not feel confined by it. It is offered as a suggested framework for conducting a pastoral assessment and each individual pastoral counselor needs to approach this task in ways that fit his or her own theological convictions and personal style. Further details on conducting a pastoral assessment can be found in *Strategic Pastoral Counseling: A Short-Term Structured Model.*

The final task of the encounter stage of Strategic Pastoral Counseling is achieving a mutually agreeable focus for counseling. Often this is self-evident, made immediately clear by the first expression of the parishioner. At other times parishioners will report a wide range of concerns in the first session and will have to be asked what should constitute the primary problem focus. The identification of the primary problem focus leads naturally to a formulation of goals for the counseling. These goals will sometimes be quite specific (i.e., to be able to make an informed decision about a potential job change) but will also at times be rather broad (i.e., to be able to express feelings related to an illness). As is illustrated in these examples, some goals will describe an end-point while others will describe more of a process. Maintaining this flexibility in how goals are understood is crucial if Strategic Pastoral Counseling is to be a helpful counseling approach for the broad range of situations faced by the pastoral counselor.

The Engagement Stage

The second stage of Strategic Pastoral Counseling involves the further engagement of the pastor and the one seeking help around the problems and concerns that brought them together. This is the heart of the counseling process. The major tasks of this stage are the exploration of the person's feelings, thoughts, and behavioral patterns associated with the central concerns and the development of new perspectives and strategies for coping or change.

It is important to note that the work of this stage may well begin in the first session. The model should not be interpreted in a rigid or mechanical manner. If the goals of the first stage are completed with time remaining in the first session, one can very appropriately begin to move into the tasks of this next stage. However, once the tasks of Stage 1 are completed, those associated with this second stage become the central focus. If the full five sessions of Strategic Pastoral Counseling are employed, this second stage normally provides the structure for sessions 2, 3, and 4.

The central foci for the three sessions normally associated with this stage are the feelings, thoughts, and behaviors associated with the problem presented by the person seeking help. Although these are usually intertwined, a selective focus on each, one at a time, ensures that each is adequately addressed and that all the crucial dynamics of the person's psychospiritual functioning are considered.

The reason for beginning with feelings is that this is where most people themselves begin when they come to a counselor. But this does not mean that most people know their feelings. The exploration of feelings involves encouraging people to face and express whatever it is that they are feeling, to the end that these feelings can be known and then dealt with appropriately. The goal at this point is to listen and respond empathically to the feelings of those seeking help, not to try to change them.

After an exploration of the major feelings being experienced by the person seeking help, the next task is an exploration of the thoughts associated with these feelings and the development of alternative ways of understanding present experiences. It is in this phase of Strategic Pastoral Counseling that the explicit use of Scripture is usually most appropriate. Bearing in mind the potential misuses and problems that can be associated with such use of religious resources, the pastoral counselor should be, nonetheless, open to a direct presentation of scriptural truths when they offer the possibility of a new and helpful perspective on one's situation.

The final task of the engagement stage of Strategic Pastoral Counseling grows directly out of this work on understanding and involves the exploration of the behavioral components of the person's functioning. Here the pastor explores what concrete things the person is doing in the face of the problems or distressing situations being encountered and together with the parishioner begins to identify changes in behavior that may be desirable. The goal of this stage is to identify changes that both pastor and parishioner agree are important and to begin to establish concrete strategies for making these changes.

The Disengagement Stage

The last session or two involves preparation for the termination of counseling and includes two specific tasks: the evaluation of progress and assessment of remaining concerns, and making arrangements regarding a referral if this is needed.

The evaluation of progress is usually a process that both pastor and parishioner will find rewarding. Some of this may be done during previous sessions. Even when this is the case, it is a good idea to use the last session to undertake a brief review of what has been learned from the counseling. Closely associated with this, of course, is an identification of remaining concerns. Seldom is everything resolved after five sessions. This means that the parishioner is preparing to leave counseling with some work yet to be done. But he or she does so with plans for the future and the development of these is an important task of the disengagement stage of Strategic Pastoral Counseling.

If significant problems remain at this point, the last couple of sessions should also be used to make referral arrangements. Ideally these should be discussed in the second or third session and they should by now be all arranged. It might even be ideal if by this point the parishioner could have had a first session with the new counselor, thus allowing a processing of this first experience as part of the final pastoral counseling session.

Recognition of one's own limitations of time, experience, training, and ability is an indispensable component of the practice of all professionals. Pastors are no exception. Pastors offering Strategic Pastoral Counseling need, therefore, to be aware of the resources within their community and be prepared to refer parishioners for help that they can better receive elsewhere.

In the vast majority of cases, the actual termination of a Strategic Pastoral Counseling relationship goes very smoothly. Most often both pastor and parishioner agree that there is no further need to meet and they find easy agreement with, even if some sadness around, the decision to discontinue the counseling sessions. However, there may be times when this process is somewhat difficult. This will sometimes be due to the parishioner's desire to continue to meet. At other times the difficulty in terminating will reside within the pastor. Regardless, the best course of action is usually to follow through on the initial limits agreed upon by both parties.

The exception to this rule is a situation where the parishioner is facing some significant stress or crisis at the end of the five sessions and where there are no other available resources to provide the support needed. If this is the situation, an extension of a few sessions may be appropriate. However, this should again be time-limited and should take the form of crisis management. It should not involve more sessions than is absolutely necessary to restore some degree of stability or to introduce the parishioner to other people who can be of assistance.

Conclusion

Strategic Pastoral Counseling provides a framework for pastors who seek to counsel in a way that is congruent with the rest of their pastoral responsibilities, psychologically informed, and responsible. While skill in implementing the model comes only over time, because the approach is focused and time-limited it is quite possible for most pastors to acquire these skills. However, counseling skills cannot be adequately learned simply by reading books. As with all interpersonal skills, they must be learned through practice, and ideally, this practice is best acquired in a context of supervisory feedback from a more experienced pastoral counselor.

The pastor who has mastered the skills of Strategic Pastoral Counseling is in a position to proclaim the Word of God in a highly personalized and relevant manner to people who are often desperate for help. This is a unique and richly rewarding opportunity. Rather than scattering seed in a broadcast manner across ground that is often stony and hard even if at places it is also fertile and receptive to growth, the pastoral counselor has the opportunity to carefully plant one seed at a time. Knowing the soil conditions, he or she is also able to plant it in a highly individualized manner, taking pains to ensure that it will not be quickly blown away, and then gently watering and nourishing its growth. This is the unique opportunity for the ministry of Strategic Pastoral Counseling. It is my prayer that pastors will see the centrality of counseling to their call to ministry, feel encouraged by the presence of an approach to pastoral counseling that lies within their skills and time availability, and will take up these responsibilities with renewed vigor and clarity of direction.

1

THE MYTHS OF ANGER

Summary: This chapter takes a brief interaction between a church member and his pastor and discusses how these short discussions can be utilized to aid our understanding of the person and their problems. The pastor is provided with an access point to help formulate some tentative hypotheses. As is often the case, some of the early statements made by the church member reflect myths about anger. Understanding these myths may provide inroads to both assessing and treating the problem.

Church Bulletin Announcement

ANGER: MINE AND YOURS
A Five-Week Series on the Bible and Anger
Starting Next Week: Sunday, February 8th, 6:00 P.M.
Pastor Harvey will lead the discussion.

Following the service in which he saw the above announcement, Bill approached Pastor Harvey and the following conversation ensued.

Bill: Well, you're going to do a series on anger, are you? Five weeks seems like a lot of time to deal with that subject. I thought the Bible only said it was wrong and sinful, and that we shouldn't feel that way!

Pastor: You and a lot of others think that, Bill. It's surprising, but there is much that we can learn from the Scriptures about anger. *(With a chuckle)* I'm not sure five weeks will be enough time. If this topic interests you or touches your life in some way, I'd sure be happy if you came and participated.

Bill: Oh, I have more than a passing interest. I struggle with anger quite a bit, actually.

Pastor: You fit right in with the rest of us, then. But, we do struggle in different ways. . . .

Bill: That's for sure. When I was younger, I just let it all out and sometimes that wasn't pleasant. As I matured, I tried to talk myself out of it when it came over me. Since becoming a Christian, I've become more confused. I try to forgive people, but sometimes my anger is so intense I think I'll break something. I don't know if it is a spiritual problem or maybe just psychological. I don't know! Joy has a real problem with my anger and she sees more of it than others. When we saw your bulletin announcement, we agreed that maybe this is for us.

Pastor: Well, I hope I can provide some biblical basis for looking at the issues. But, you know, sometimes it is helpful to talk one on one with someone who can help you talk through the issues specific to your concerns. Ever thought about doing that? Perhaps after the series you would have some good foundational understanding to build on in dealing with it in a personal way. In fact, maybe you and Joy would benefit from doing that together.

Bill, who is thirty-seven years old, has been a Christian for five years and works as a supervisor in a local manufacturing plant. Both he and his wife Joy, thirty-four years old, made personal commitments to Christ through an Evangelism Explosion outreach and have attended church regularly since. They have begun teaching Sunday school. They have two children, seven-year-old Jeremy and two-year-old Shannon. Bill played and coached hockey during his teens and twenties and still plays occasionally. Joy is at home for the children and is a creative homemaker, although she was in the workplace before Jeremy was born.

In the church bulletin announcement, anger is expressed in both nonjudgmental terms and in terms that suggest it is the experience of all. Thus it is not the problem of some select, more depraved individuals. It is important to remember that announcements and titles communicate something about a topic.

The pastor is suggesting that Bill's assumptions about what the Bible has to say are universal, not peculiar to him. Likewise, Bill is identified with "the rest of us." This is an important principle. Those who feel isolated in their problems frequently become trapped in the despair of assuming no one else struggles as they do and, therefore, no one could understand them. The movement from personalizing our pain as unique to a perspective that acknowledges our pain as part of the universal experience in a broken world is important. It is the movement from the isolated individual in pain to the individual in community where pain is experienced by all in a world broken by sin. The form of suffering and pain may vary from person to person, but the fact of suffering is common to all. As I stand with all in suffering, so I may stand with all in healing. The pastor is implying this when he acknowledges common experience alongside differing forms of expressing and experiencing.

It is important to note that the pastor lightens the subject with a chuckle and expresses an invitation and a desire for Bill's participation. He is expressing hope that he may be of help which may reduce any assumption that he has all the answers and that Bill's participative involvement is necessary and, thus, Bill shares responsibility for the outcome. He also is bringing some realism in suggesting the series may be only part of the solution and that dealing with personal issues in a more confidential setting may be an option to consider. He is also taking some of the emphasis off of Bill by suggesting that both he and Joy should consider such counseling.

Formulating Tentative Hypotheses

In pastoral ministry people often reveal a lot about themselves in brief interactions at the back of the church. This information needs to be seen as part of the encounter stage in that we are becoming acquainted with the person and their concerns and are attempting to formulate tentative hypotheses. However, a number of cautions need to be kept in mind.

1. Approach these interactions with a compassionate heart and a listening ear. Do not use them as an opportunity to go after information in a direct and intrusive manner. The pastor made a simple comment about the length of time for the series and asked Bill whether this was an area he was interested in. This unobtrusive response elicited a fair bit of information. Resist the temptation to engage the person fully at this point. Not only will there be excessive interruptions at the back of the church, but you run the risk of being superficial in your responses.

2. Recognize that the encounter stage is focused on data collection and the formulation of an assessment or diagnosis. All information is important at this stage, even the information that is revealed in these initial brief interactions. Process what the person said. How did they frame the problem? What is their reaction to the problem? What are they looking for? Are there myths surrounding the difficulties they are experiencing? Your tentative answers to these questions will aid your preparation before the first session.

3. Rather than focusing on the details of what was said, look for themes and patterns. If you had to summarize in one sentence, what is the person saying about their problem? (i.e. "Basically she wants me to talk to her son so he will stop doing drugs" or "He wants to talk to me about his career because he has been offered a job and needs to decide by tomorrow.") Remember, at this stage these are hunches and hypotheses, not definitive conclusions. However, they may prove to be valuable later on.

In seeking to respond in helpful ways to those to whom we would minister, it is important to be intentional and aware of our processing of information shared with us. Keen observation and intense listening will lead to the formation of *tentative hypotheses*. These become *working hypotheses* for clarifying and defining the issues to be dealt with. The conversation with Bill has provided us with some potential areas to be explored.

1. The interaction between Bill and Joy is the place where anger is acted out and experienced as painful or uncomfortable.
2. Bill has tried *expression* as a mode of dealing with his anger but that left something to be desired.
3. Bill has tried *suppression* and that, too, did not seem to work. It does not appear at this point that *repression* is something Bill may be aware of as a possibility.
4. Bill has come to think of anger in a right/wrong dichotomy, concluding that anger is, simply, wrong and something we shouldn't experience.
5. Bill feels there is a relationship between forgiveness and anger, but his attempt at "spiritual" solutions has not seemed to work. Therefore, maybe it is only psychological, but what is the relationship between what is spiritual and what is psychological?
6. The intensity of his anger is frightening to Bill and he may fear loss of control.

The purpose in generating many hypotheses is to avoid a myopia that may come from leaping to a single conclusion or explanation and assure that one will be open to a wide range of possible explanations and understandings of Bill's experience with anger. One must be led by an openness to hearing all that Bill is saying, but not limited to his personal understanding of his experience. However, that is often the only place to begin if one is to communicate acceptance and provide a nonthreatening and safe environment in which Bill can explore new ways of understanding and responding to his experience.

The Access Point in a Helping Relationship

Such casual contacts, as we see illustrated in this case, are very important. If we bring intentionality and some principles into them, we increase the potential for moving people toward significant growth. We may identify a significant *access point* into the individual's life and struggle. An access point is the doorway someone provides for you to engage them. It will normally be the point at which they feel safe to begin a relationship in which they see some potential for assistance. It may not, in fact, be the central or even a significant factor, but rather the person's point of comfort in relation to you or the problem as they are experiencing it at that moment.

In certain contexts, people may be more comfortable to begin at a *spiritual access point,* as was the case with Bill. At other times, a *physical access point* may come from sharing with a medical doctor. In such a case, Bill might have focused on the discomfort in his stomach or tightness in his chest or some other symptom. On the other hand, a *psychological access point* may be to talk of the depression that he experiences or the relational tension. There are many access points that may provide doorways into the human soul. We enter into the lives of people at their invitation through the doorway they provide, but we must be aware that the issue will manifest itself in every dimension of the person's being, not just the one dimension or dimensions which they are able to identify at the moment. The symptom the person chooses to provide as the access point may not be the key issue, but only a place to start.

Satir speaks of levels or domains where access may be achieved as including physical, intellectual, emotional, sensual, interactional, contextual, nutritional, or spiritual (Satir, 1982). The access point is the geographical point on the map of the person's life where you begin the journey with them. The domains are interactive and dynamic. Such breadth of perspective provides both a caution and an openness to the process of dealing with the presenting symptom and implies a multidisciplinary understanding of both pain and healing.

It is respectful on the part of the helper to accept the access point as relevant and as an invitation, while recognizing that it is only a place to start. The access point is determined by factors such as: the idiosyncratic definition of the presenting problem; the pain threshold personal to the individual; availability of help; the family history of problem definition; and cultural factors that determine "acceptable" problems and where or if it is appropriate to deal with them.

It may be helpful to expand on these access points briefly. The *physical* will normally focus on symptoms or health issues. In our culture, there is often freedom to focus on more or less clearly defined medical issues. However, this may lead to a blind spot in seeing the problem in terms of other contributing factors. The *intellectual* approach may define problems in terms of confused thinking, difficulty in recall, irrationality, "crazy thoughts," delusional thinking, or sad thoughts. The person may define their concern in any of these ways. Some may focus on *emotional* dimensions such as depression, sad feelings, anger, weeping, manic states, or phobias that they may be conscious of in themselves. The *sensual* access point is less common and usually occurs with aesthetically oriented people who may focus on feelings of pleasure or discomfort, or they may use imagery or analogy to present their state, often indirectly. Persons who focus on the *interactional* dimensions of life will focus on relational conflict with people in their lives. They may have a great need either to overbond or please, or to avoid others in withdrawal. They may experience fear in the relational sphere of their lives. Some will focus on the *contextual* aspects such as environmental, organizational, or social rather than personal aspects of the problem. There may be a sense of victimhood as they react to the impact of what is in their life context and sometimes they may not see their personal input to issues. A *nutritional* entry point would focus on the role of food and the impact that it has on contributing to the sense of nonwell-being that the person is experiencing. For people who approach life with a *spiritual* perspective, the focus may be on defining the issues in moral terms, as a loss of faith, the presence of doubt, a sense of abandonment by God, guilt, loss of meaning, and so on.

The important issue for the counselor is to be aware that the presenting problem is only an entry point, to be respected and honored, but not immediately accepted as the most important or only dimension that needs to be addressed in the counseling.

Understanding Myths

Even in the short exchange with the pastor, Bill has communicated a number of his thoughts and feelings about anger.

1. The Bible does not have much to say about anger.
2. All anger is sin.
3. Anger and forgiveness are unrelated.
4. Anger is either a psychological or spiritual issue.
5. Anger is caused by circumstances or other people.
6. Anger is resolved in one way.
7. Anger is resolved by getting it off your chest.

A careful processing of this list will reveal that most of these statements are myths about the topic of anger. It is quite possible that Bill's problems with anger revolve around his beliefs and values on the topic so it is important to think through each of them carefully. In Bill's case there are seven myths, and at this point it is not clear which of them will be the most salient in terms of resolution. In other situations, you may find that people only share one or two myths when they make initial contact. The bottom line is that this early stage of encounter is very important to the entire counseling process and should not be undervalued, even though it is brief.

Myth 1: The Bible Does Not Have Much to Say about Anger

It is intriguing that many Christians are in the same camp as Bill. Somehow they have not been able to link the biblical data with their own experience of anger. However, a cursory reading of the Bible will reveal that anger is a key theme in Scripture. Whether it is God's experience of anger or its presence between individuals, the term "anger" is utilized 390 times in the New International Version of the biblical record. This is filled out even further by terms like "wrath" (197 times), "provoke" (52 times), and "vengeance" (32 times).

God's Anger

The phrase that captures God's anger the best is "wrath of God." This is not a fashionable teaching in many contemporary churches because it appears, at least to us, to be in marked contrast to God's love. As a result we have a natural propensity to favor the latter and downplay the former. However, these two attributes of God need to be seen in tandem. It is because God loves and cares for us that he reacts with wrath when his people sin against him and break his covenant. In fact, the wilderness experience of the people of Israel reflects this reaction.

> The LORD's anger burned against Israel and he made them wander in the desert forty years, until the whole generation of those who had done evil in his sight was gone. (Num. 32:13)

The prophetic image of the day of the Lord takes the concept of God's wrath even further. It is a warning not just to Israel but all nations that divine anger will not be spared.

> The great day of the LORD is near—near and coming quickly. Listen! The cry on the day of the LORD will be bitter, the shouting of the warrior there. That day will be a day of wrath. (Zeph. 1:14–15a)

Because of our own experience we tend to project human qualities onto God and assume that his anger is like our children's temper tantrums in that it is uncontrolled and contains no love or mercy. But God is compassionate and patient. In fact, the Hebrew word for "patient" literally means "length of wrath." And so these divine attributes blend together.

> The LORD is compassionate and gracious, slow to anger, abounding in love. He will not always accuse, nor will he harbor his anger forever. (Ps. 103:8–9)

This Old Testament theme is picked up in the New Testament when God's anger is placed in contrast to eternal life and the gospel.

> Whoever believes in the Son has eternal life, but whoever rejects the Son will not see life, for God's wrath remains on him. (John 3:36)

> Since we have now been justified by his blood, how much more shall we be saved from God's wrath through him! (Rom. 5:9)

Humanity in its natural state before God is in sin and because of that, God's wrath is the natural consequence. God hates sin and his holiness will not allow it. The only antidote is eternal life found through a relationship with Jesus Christ, the one who experienced God's wrath on the cross. The gospel, then, has the power to overcome sin and to avert the wrath of God. But what of those who are sinning currently? If God is angry with them, why are they not experiencing it? If God's wrath is on them, why is it not obvious? It almost appears that sin has no consequences at present.

> The wrath of God is being revealed from heaven against all the godlessness and wickedness of men who suppress the truth by their wickedness. . . . Therefore God gave them over in the sinful desires of their hearts to sexual impurity. . . . God gave them over to shameful lusts. . . . he gave them over to a depraved mind. . . . (Rom. 1:18, 24, 26, 28)

The teaching of Romans 1 makes it clear that God's wrath is being revealed at the present time. While it is not the full and complete culmination of his anger, it is being expressed. How? By God allowing people to pursue their own course, their own desires, and their own wishes. God's "hands off" approach to sin is his way of expressing anger and wrath. In giving people over to their own sin, God allows them to experience the natural consequences of the sinful life, consequences that are neither honoring to God nor pleasant for humanity. Ironically, his anger in the present is displayed with a type of passivity, a rather marked contrast to what will happen in the future.

> He, too, will drink of the wine of God's fury, which has been poured full strength into the cup of his wrath. He will be tormented with burning sulfur in the presence of the holy angels and of the Lamb. (Rev. 14:10)

Anger at God

The experience of Jonah is an intriguing example of anger at God because the Creator did not do what the created thought he should do! Jonah had avoided going to Nineveh, but eventually, after a slight detour, he preached the message of impending destruction. God, however, "had compassion and did not bring upon them the destruction he had threatened" (Jonah 3:10). Jonah was angry to the point that he asked God to take his life. God's question to him is a penetrating one: "Have you any right to be angry?" (Jonah 4:4) and he follows it up by teaching him the contrast between divine compassion and that experienced by Jonah.

Although the word "anger" is not used, it is clear that Job's communication with God is filled with this kind of feeling. He cannot understand why God is allowing this experience and he expresses himself with poignant feeling.

> I cry out to you, O God, but you do not answer; I stand up, but you merely look at me. You turn on me ruthlessly; with the might of your hand you attack me. (Job 30:20–21)

The psalmist has a similar experience as he struggles with the prosperity of the wicked. The word is not used, but his sentiments seem to reflect an underlying frustration and anger.

> They have no struggles; their bodies are healthy and strong. They are free from the burdens common to man; they are not plagued

by human ills. . . . Surely in vain I have kept my heart pure; in vain have I washed my hands in innocence. (Ps. 73:4–5, 13)

A similar sentiment is expressed when David experiences God being distant.

Why, O Lord, do you stand far off? Why do you hide yourself in times of trouble? (Ps. 10:1)

Anger and the Old Testament

There are a number of words for anger, wrath, and fury in the Old Testament. *Anaph* means to snort or blow through the nostrils and is used to describe God's anger. This is the word that the psalmist uses in Psalm 2:12: "Kiss the Son, lest he be angry and you be destroyed in your way." Almost all the uses of this word refer to the nature of God's anger.

Charah and its derivatives communicate a type of anger that is burning, heated, or passionate. Interestingly, this physiologically oriented description of anger is linked with God and humans. It is the word that is used to describe Jonah's anger at God (Jonah 4:1, 4, 9), as well as Nehemiah's anger at the social injustice that God's people were experiencing (Neh. 5:6).

Qatsaph is linked with a sense of wroth or displeasure with others. It is used to describe Moses' anger at Eleazar and Ithamar when they burned the goat in the sin offering (Lev. 10:16).

Provocation and sadness is communicated by the word *kaas*. It is the word used in Proverbs 12:16: "A fool shows his annoyance at once, but a prudent man overlooks an insult."

The Proverbs provide wisdom on the topic of human anger. These verses reflect the dangers that are inherent in poorly managed anger:

A wise man fears the Lord and shuns evil, but a fool is hotheaded and reckless. (14:16)

A quick-tempered man does foolish things, and a crafty man is hated. (14:17)

A patient man has great understanding, but a quick-tempered man displays folly. (14:29)

A gentle answer turns away wrath, but a harsh word stirs up anger. (15:1)

A hot-tempered man stirs up dissension, but a patient man calms a quarrel. (15:18)

A man of knowledge uses words with restraint, and a man of understanding is even-tempered. (17:27)

A hot-tempered man must pay the penalty; if you rescue him, you will have to do it again. (19:19)

Do not make friends with a hot-tempered man, do not associate with one easily angered, or you may learn his ways and get yourself ensnared. (22:24–25)

A fool gives full vent to his anger, but a wise man keeps himself under control. (29:11)

An angry man stirs up dissension, and a hot-tempered one commits many sins. (29:22)

For as churning the milk produces butter, and as twisting the nose produces blood, so stirring up anger produces strife. (30:33)

Anger and the New Testament

The four main Greek words for anger in the New Testament are *thumos, parorgismos, orge,* and *aganaktesis. Thumos* anger is a turbulent, boiling commotion that can be best illustrated by the lighting of a match. At the point where the match ignites, there is an explosion of the flame. This is *thumos* anger. We experience it as temper or rage. It is referred to in Scripture as "fits of rage" (Gal. 5:20) or "rage" (Eph. 4:31), and is also used to describe God's wrath (Rev. 14:10, 19).[i]

Anger that demonstrates itself in irritation or exasperation is captured in the Greek word *parorgismos.* When Paul is writing to parents in Ephesians he encourages them not to "exasperate your children" (6:4). In other words, do not have a style of discipline that disempowers children and makes them frustrated. To do this is to "embitter" and "discourage" them (Col. 3:21). This is not the boiling, turbulent commotion of *thumos* anger but the internal experience of irritation that occurs in the presence of others' behavior. It was what Paul describes Moses as feeling when he witnessed the idol worship of the people of Israel (Rom. 10:19).[ii]

The third type of anger is of another quality altogether. *Orge* is a settled inner attitude that may, but not necessarily, lead to revenge and personal animosity. This is the most complex of the three words because it can only be understood in its biblical context. For example, when Jesus was going to heal the man with the shriveled hand, the Pharisees were concerned that this was being done on the Sabbath. Jesus "looked around at them in anger [*orge*] and, deeply distressed at their stubborn hearts, said to the man, 'Stretch out your hand'" (Mark 3:5). In contrast Paul admonishes the Ephesian Christians to "get rid of all bitterness, rage [*thumos*] and anger [*orge*], brawling and slander, along with every form of malice" (Eph. 4:31). In the first case, Jesus reacted to religious stubbornness in anger but there was no revenge or personal animosity. In the second case, Paul recognizes that *orge* can move into personal animosity and not reflect a life of righteousness.[iii]

Aganaktesis has the sense of irritation and indignation with a component of grief. When the disciples were not responding well to the children that were being brought to him, Jesus was "indignant" (Mark 10:14). When Paul distinguishes worldly sorrow and godly sorrow in 2 Corinthians 7, he describes the latter as producing "indignation" (v. 11). The emphasis of this word revolves around annoyance at something done by someone else.[iv]

Only used once in the New Testament, *cholao* is connected with the word "gall" in the sense of bitterness of feeling. Jesus is instructing the Jews and refers to their anger (*cholao*) in healing the man on the Sabbath day (John 7:23).

In sum, it is clear that Bill's sense that the Bible does not have much to say about anger is a myth. The pastor could easily take much longer than five weeks to cover this material alone!

Myth 2: All Anger Is Sin

Bill's assessment of the morality of anger is very typical of many evangelicals. There is a fundamental assumption that all anger is wrong and sinful and ought to be purged from our lives. Such a claim may reflect the fact that anger is difficult to manage and control. Also, many people have been on the receiving end of angry outbursts that have left them feeling threatened and intimidated. On the other hand, some of the secular literature on the topic focuses on the validity of human experience and in the process runs the risk of setting the morality issue aside. For example, in her very helpful book *The Dance of Anger* Harriet Goldhor Lerner says:

> "Is my anger legitimate?" "Do I have a right to be angry?" "What's the use of my getting angry?" "What good will it do?" These questions can be excellent ways of silencing ourselves and shutting off our anger. Let us question these questions. Anger is neither legitimate nor illegitimate, meaningful or pointless. Anger simply is. To ask, "Is my anger legitimate?" is similar to asking, "Do I have a right to be thirsty? After all, I just had a glass of water fifteen minutes ago. Surely my thirst is not legitimate. And besides, what's the point of getting thirsty when I can't get anything to drink now, anyway?" (Lerner, 1985)

In the presence of these two extreme views—one that emphasizes only the sinful component of anger and the other that puts anger into the same moral category as thirst—pastors and their parishioners need to grapple with the rightness and wrongness of anger.

First, we need to recognize that God experiences anger. It is part of his character. It is one of his attributes. His capacity to react to the sin of others is resident in who he is. Jesus demonstrated that in his pilgrimage on earth. He was not immune from the intense experience of anger, nor was he unwilling to express it. While the term "anger" is not utilized in John 2:12–16, it is clear that when Jesus made a whip out of cords, drove the money changers and their animals out of the temple, and turned their tables upside down, he was experiencing an intense experience of frustration and anger. When you read the words, "Get these out of here! How dare you turn my Father's house into a market!" (John 2:16), you can hear deep passion over a value that has been violated.

Is it possible that our human experience of anger reflects the image of God in us? The fact that we are able to react with passion and candor in the presence of sin and wrongdoing may be traceable to divine qualities. On the other hand, our tendency toward passivity and lack of expression, particularly in the face of others' actions, may reflect our lack of spiritual and psychological sensitivity.

The biblical record does not condemn all anger as sin, nor does it affirm all anger as valid and acceptable. The clearest statement on this issue is found in Ephesians 4:26–27.

> "In your anger do not sin": Do not let the sun go down while you are still angry, and do not give the devil a foothold.

The first phrase communicates a distinction between being angry and sinning. On the one hand, you can be angry, while on the other, you can sin or not sin in that state. The meaning of this becomes much clearer when we understand that Paul uses the word *orge*. In your *orge* anger, an anger that is characterized by a settled inner attitude, do not sin. In other words, this anger, which has the potential for revenge and personal animosity, can turn into sin. It is not the feeling of anger that is the problem here; it is what you do with it. The sin is linked more with personal animosity and vengeance than with anger.

Some couples have taken the next phrase and turned it into an injunction to stay up late to resolve their marital squabbles! The argument is simple. The Bible says you should not let the sun go down on your wrath so we should not go to sleep until we have resolved all of our feelings. Clarifying and moving on from conflict is hard enough, but this so-called biblical injunction adds further pressure. But this is not what Paul is driving at in the passage. We need to recognize that a different word for anger is employed in the second phrase. The anger that is linked with the sun going down is *parorgismos*. It is not that all conflicts need to be resolved before bed, but that the nurturing of *orge* anger may turn it into *parorgismos*. Appropriate anger may turn into sin by the cultivation of the feelings that will precipitate irritation and exasperation and eventually evolve into bitterness.

The final phrase in these two verses—"and do not give the devil a foothold"—can almost seem like an afterthought that is unrelated to what preceded it. However, these three phrases are very much intertwined. If anger moves into sin through a nurturing process that creates irritation and exasperation with resultant bitterness, we are giving the devil an inroad into our lives. In contemporary evangelical thinking, there is a significant amount of discussion about the role of the demonic. In this context, the biblical record links the demonic with how one manages his or her anger. The word used to describe this process is "foothold."

When we used to play squash, both of us tried to utilize the T-line to our advantage. The T-line is located about three-quarters of the way back in the court. If you stay close to that line, you are able to run to almost any spot on the court without difficulty. On the other hand, if you can get your opponent off the T-line, you can drop a shot in the opposite end of the court so he has trouble returning it. Fundamentally, each player needs to be committed to staying close to the T-line. To move away from it is to give your fellow competitor a "foothold." This is precisely what Paul is describing in this passage. If you do not handle anger properly, you are moving away from the T-line and giving the devil an opportunity to make a point.

These two verses provide the touchstone for all the biblical material on anger. Bill has concluded that anger is wrong and sinful, but he is only partially accurate. Depending on the situation that provokes it and the disposition of the person experiencing it, anger may be righteous or it may be sinful.

Myth 3: Anger and Forgiveness Are Unrelated

Bill has expressed the sentiment that he has tried to forgive people, but he still experiences anger. This almost gives the impression that they are unrelated issues; you can forgive someone, but still experience anger with them. This link is an important one and our understanding of it is rooted in our understanding of God's forgiveness. We have already established that God's wrath abides on those who have not experienced his forgiveness. In contrast, forgiveness leads to a substantially different experience.

> Blessed is he whose transgressions are forgiven, whose sins are covered. Blessed is the man whose sin the LORD does not count against him and in whose spirit is no deceit. (Ps. 32:1–2)

When Nathan confronted David over his sin with Bathsheba and Uriah, the King was seemingly oblivious to all that had happened. But when the truth did sink in and he became aware of the consequences of his behavior, he was able to go through a period of mourning and repentance and then enter into a fresh sense of forgiveness. The forgiveness, as enunciated in Psalm 32, was characterized by four qualities:

1. Forgiveness is a divine response that is resident in God, not in the individual's behavior. Sin demands justice and payment. If God had given David what he deserved, forgiveness would never have been granted.
2. A lack of forgiveness is demonstrated in holding the sin against the other person. They may be reminded of it directly or it may be nurtured in the mind of the offended party. Forgiveness covers the sin so that it is not held against the person. Both literally and metaphorically, it is covered.
3. True forgiveness means that the forensic issues are dealt with. A forgiven person does not have to pay for their sin. Judicially, they stand before God with a sense of being justified, cleared, and as "good as new." They can rest in the assurance that their past sins will not be counted against them.
4. Forgiveness is also motivating and cleansing. When the psalmist describes himself as experiencing an absence of deceit in his spirit, he is capturing the results of being forgiven. There is no longer a need to hide and cover up due

to a fear of being caught or punished. Genuine transparency can occur both within and without because the sins of the past have been resolved. This cleansing then becomes a motivator to live with integrity before God.

What does all of this have to do with anger? Let's reflect on the case of Judy. Her eight-year-old daughter was killed in a car accident after they were hit by a drunk driver. These events provoke many emotional reactions, with anger being one of the most dominant. How does Judy deal with her anger? How does it tie to forgiveness? Can she forgive and forget? First, we need to assert that the presence of normal brain functioning makes it impossible to forget. Judy will always remember that fateful day until the day she dies. To ask her not to remember it is to request a physiologically impossible task. As long as we have a memory, most events, particularly the significant ones, will be accessible to us.

Does it make sense that Judy is angry? Her sense of injustice, loss, grief, trauma, and betrayal will be great. We should expect her initial response to be one of anger. She will find it easy to demand justice and payment. Vengeance will be a natural by-product and she will want to hold the drunk driver's sin against him. She will find it natural to make him accountable to her, rather than seeing him as accountable to God, and in the process she will experience an emotional block inside that will defile her spirit. But the question is: Will she be able to get to the place of forgiving the drunk driver?

At times, well-intentioned Christians will advise people like Judy, shortly after an event like this, to write a letter to the drunk driver and tell him that she has forgiven him. If she is still numb from the experience, she may find it easy to be compliant and people will be pleased that she has come through such a horrendous time and has forgiven in spite of it. However, until she has experienced the full impact of his sin, she will not be able to grant true forgiveness. The depth of forgiveness is understood best through an appreciation of the depth of sin. Often this can only occur with the mediating role of anger. God's forgiveness of us is the best example of this.

The horrific nature of Calvary is a testament to the horror of sin. Calvary is not a minimization or trivialization of sin. It is not a form of cheap forgiveness. Calvary is not simply a special event that made it possible for us to go to heaven. Rather, it is the full display of God's wrath against our sin. Paul captures this in Galatians when he argues that:

> "Cursed is everyone who does not continue to do everything written in the Book of the Law." . . . Christ redeemed us from the curse of the law by becoming a curse for us, for it is written: "Cursed is everyone who is hung on a tree." (Gal. 3:10, 13)

Christ's death and the resultant forgiveness flowed out of God's anger at sin, an anger that was displayed at his Son on the cross. Anger and forgiveness were not separated, but the former was needed in order to get to the latter. God's love and his justice were blended perfectly to accomplish our salvation. Calvary is not just a statement about forgiveness; it is a loud statement on sin.

To accomplish what needs to occur in her healing process, Judy needs to experience the impact of her loss. In that experience, anger will come to the surface. Her natural response will be to want justice and payment and vengeance. She will want to make the driver accountable to her. But in that struggle she will need to come to understand the freeing nature of forgiveness. The wound will not go away, but the poison coming out of it will cease. The accident will always be present, but the emotional trauma that goes with it will subside.

Does this happen all at once? Normally forgiveness has three components. There is the moment of forgiveness that comes after a process of anger and frustration, which has taught us the full impact of the event. Then there is the ongoing work that is required to still live consistent with the forgiveness that has been granted. Forgiveness demands that we respond appropriately to the other party and make a behavioral commitment to demonstrate the love of Christ. Finally, there is the recognition that our existence in the body at present renders all our moral choices to be influenced by sin and frailty. Only in our future heavenly state will we be able to fully, completely, and absolutely give and receive forgiveness. Until then we live between Christ's first and second advent, recognizing that forgiveness is hard work and usually involves an experience of anger. Bill may need to understand the intricacies of this link in more detail.

Myth 4: Anger Is Either a Psychological or a Spiritual Issue

One of the main reasons anger is so difficult to understand and manage is that it involves so many facets of our lives. It is simplistic to argue that anger relates to either spiritual issues or psychological issues; it is much more comprehensive than that. The P-R-E-A-C-H-E-S acrostic will aid us in our delineation of anger. While the access points represent the area of awareness or comfort that the person has in presenting their problem, the current acrostic represents the counselor's attempt both to understand the extent of the problem and to broaden the counselee's perspective to realize that anger has many dimensions.

Anger is a **P**hysical process. In fact, a recent book edited by Kassinove (1995) summarizes the psychophysiological effects of anger in the cardiovascular system in terms of pulse rate, systolic blood pressure, and diastolic blood pressure.

Anger is a **R**elational issue. Anger is a way of expressing displeasure with others and what they have done. It is a way of exerting power and influence. It is a way of functioning in community. It is a way, both its dark side and light side, of relating to other people and to God.

Anger is an **E**motion. It is passionate and intense. It is a powerful feeling that at times seems to overwhelm us. Quite apart from our expression of it, our experience of anger is an emotional one. And it is in this experience that we often are confused.

Anger often involves **A**ction. Sometimes when we are angry we withdraw. At other times we sulk and manipulate. We may express it or confess it. We may suppress it or repress it. But we usually do something with it. Rarely is anger simply a feeling that is present.

Anger involves our **C**ognitions. It is more than something we feel. It involves our thoughts, our values, our beliefs. When we get angry we are thinking about injustice, violation, broken promises, and thwarted expectations.

Anger is often related to our **H**istory. Particularly for those with chronic anger, the baggage of the past may be influencing the responses of the present. Current situations may stimulate old responses, and many of those historical patterns of responding are well entrenched and hard to break.

Anger is very much tied to our **E**nvironment. Circumstances and situations in our personal world will stimulate anger. At times an event will occur in the world that will elicit an angry response. While our experience of anger is within, the source of it seems at times outside of ourselves.

Anger is an issue that is **S**piritual. With the vast amount of biblical data, it would be impossible to see anger in any other way. God experiences anger. We, too, experience it, at times in a way that is consistent with holiness and righteousness, and at other times in ways that are more in harmony with sin and frailty.

Is Bill right when he suggests that anger is either psychological or spiritual? No, anger is comprehensive and it is only with this understanding that we will be able to bring help and healing to those who are struggling.

Myth 5: Anger Is Caused by Circumstances or Other People

Sarah stops you at the door after the morning service and she is very upset. In a hostile, adversarial tone she blurts out, "Why do you refer to unbelievers as unchurched and seekers? I am tired of the way we beat around the bush with non-Christians. If they do not have Christ they are going to hell! Why don't you tell them straight?" You are torn between responding at length to this angry outburst, trying not to create a scene, or making sure the other two hundred people can shake your hand! Later on that day you reflect on what happened and ask a key question: Who/what is responsible for Sarah's anger? Is it your terminology? Is it a theological/biblical issue? Is it something unrelated to what transpired in the service? In pastoral ministry these questions are extremely important because our answers to them will be reflected in our attempts at resolution.

Many of the phrases that we use when we are angry unveil our position on the responsibility question:

"She makes my blood boil!"
"He gets under my skin!"
"Every time I see him I get furious!"
"I find my Dad infuriating!"

All of these phrases allocate blame and fault elsewhere. Someone else has created/caused/facilitated my anger, and I am not responsible. While such a position may make sense experientially, it is not conducive to helping people. In experiencing Sarah's "blame shifting" mode, the pastor might be tempted to drop all references to the unchurched and to seekers. Since these phrases have "caused" her anger the only way she is going to "feel better" is to have the stimulus that produced her response removed. Most pastors understand the futility of such a response. If we ceased particular activities every time they upset someone, we might end up closing down completely!

The corollary to the "blame game" approach in anger is to ignore any of the stimuli that may have precipitated the anger and to hold the person experiencing the intense feelings fully responsible. From there they can be told that they have no right to be angry and should stop feeling it. This was the case with Rachel, who had been sexually abused by her father over a period of three years. In counseling she came to understand that she was experiencing anger as a result of this event. Some friends in her church told her that she should not be angry and that her anger was something she should deal with on her own. It did not matter what happened to her; she had no right to be angry. One wonders whether Jesus would be pleased with an injunction that asks people to react passively to the sin of others!

It would be easy to look at these two positions and ask if there are any other options. After all, if you cannot blame others and you cannot hold yourself fully responsible, what else is there? The answer is found in the nature of human relationships. Let's use marriage as an example.

Jim is a conscientious, hard-working person who always has his projects organized and completed ahead of the deadlines. His wife Julia is a procrastinator who has trouble organizing her day, much less her projects. While they have similarities in other areas, the difference in administrative concerns creates difficulty for both of them. A typical scenario would unfold just before going to bed.

Jim: Have you made that call to Heather about our appointment tomorrow?

Julia: Oh no! I forgot and it's too late to call her because they go to bed early.

Jim: I reminded you about that yesterday. How could you forget?

Julia: If it was that important to you, why didn't you make the call?

Jim: I get so tired of this. Your attitude about these things makes me mad.

Julia: Well, I get tired of always falling short of your rules.

The key question needs to be asked: Why is Jim angry? Is he angry because of the way Julia functions administratively, so she is at fault? Or is he just being picky and needs to learn a little patience and understanding, so the anger is his fault? And what about Julia? Is she angry because of Jim's rules or should she deny her frustration and get on with her life? There is a third alternative that takes it out of the blame arena. Both of them can express their anger and share their understanding without putting pressure on the other person to take full responsibility for it. This approach affirms two facts in human relationships: (1) that we are responsible for our own behavior, and (2) we cannot take responsibility for other people's reactions. A follow-up conversation may sound something like this.

Jim: Because of the kind of person I am, I assume that when I remind someone of something, they will follow up for sure. When it comes to our relationship I know this is a problem, which is made worse by the fact that I am trying to avoid embarrassment with some of our friends. When you fall down administratively, I feel like it looks bad on me and on us. I do not want that to happen so I constantly try to make you perfect in this area.

Julia: Do you know what happens for me? When this kind of thing occurs, it takes me back home. Dad used to do everything for me, but then at times he would get angry and upset because I had not completed a task. As I got older I realized it taught me to avoid taking responsibility for my own behavior. It is much easier for me to let you take over in these areas, but I want you to let me fail and experience the consequences. When you give me a job and then ask me if I have done it, I feel like you are handing me something and then taking it back. This makes me feel like a child again and that gets me angry.

Bill describes himself as angry with others and he indicates that Joy is struggling with his temper. Who is responsible for the anger? It is a myth to argue that circumstances and other people are fully responsible for our anger.

Myth 6: Anger Is Resolved in One Way

Even in Bill's brief discussion about anger, he noted a number of different strategies for handling anger: get it off my chest, talk myself out of it, and forgive others. This is a very typical response of people who come for counseling because of problems with anger. Often they are not struggling with the inner experience of anger, but more with the most helpful way to express it. At some intuitive level we all realize that anger is a part of life, but our difficulty comes with the style we utilize to manage or direct the anger. Sometimes people will choose one style, like getting it off your chest, and will come to believe that this is the only style that is appropriate. Is there only one style for resolving problems with anger?

Rob grew up in a family where anger was always verbally expressed when it was experienced. If Dad was irritated with a fellow driver he would yell out the window at them. If Mum was experiencing irritation with one of the children, she would yell at them, wherever and whenever. Rob modeled his own anger management after these examples, whether it was at school, in social situations, or at work. Two years ago Rob married Sarah. They are now going for counseling because Sarah feels that Rob is insensitive to her, or at least that is how she conceptualizes the problem. When they are at home and he is irritated with her, he will let her know in a verbally aggressive manner. His response is not influenced by the time of the day, her state of mind, or the circumstances of the moment. The reaction is immediate; if you are feeling angry, you must express it.

In recent weeks Rob has embarrassed Sarah in social situations by confronting her for something that she has done or said. Last Sunday he left the service early and was waiting in the car for her. After five minutes he could not take it any longer and marched back into the church foyer, yelled at her in front of her friends, and demanded that she come to the car immediately. Sarah arrived at the car in tears and when she questioned his response to her, he answered, "I was angry. What would you expect me to do?"

Rob has failed to understand that the experience of anger is quite distinct from the expression. Because he is feeling angry it does not necessarily follow that he needs to express it verbally. While he may have learned that style in his family of origin, this is not the only way to express what he is feeling. At times it is helpful to control the expression of anger until a more appropriate time. If it was important to let Sarah know that she made him upset, he could have done it when she arrived in the car. On the other hand, maybe he could have concluded that his experience and his expectations were selfish and inappropriate so there would have been no need to express his anger.

Most of us have learned a particular style in the expression of anger and find it difficult to break out of this pattern. We need to recognize that there is more than one way to respond to our experience of anger and that different situations demand different responses. On a given day your spouse may not come to the car on time, your teenager may come home late, your dog may get lost, you may hear of the death of a friend, and your waiter may bring your meal to the table cold. Each of these situations may elicit an inner experience of frustration and anger, but they may each demand a unique response that is appropriate to the situation.

Bill has been seeking a way to resolve his problems with anger. Through counseling he will probably come to realize that there is more than one style for facilitative resolution.

Myth 7: Anger Is Resolved by Getting It Off Your Chest

The "get it off your chest" image is physiologically based and premised on the fact that anger builds up inside you and must be released or it will build to a dangerous level. Rhonda was a person who believed in this view of anger and she often used the pastor as a "dump site" for her anger. On one particular occasion, she was incensed that he talked about sex from the pulpit on Sunday morning. She had never heard of such a thing happening in church and sat through the whole service steaming. When she came to the door her introductory comment was telling: "I need to get something off my chest!" Implicit in this statement was the fact that her need for release was inevitable. There was no way she could control the anger because it was controlling her. What was inside had to come out.

The idea that anger is inside and needs to come out to be resolved can be traced to a particular understanding of catharsis or purging. In medicine, a cathartic is a laxative that aids in the purging of the bowels. In a similar fashion, a cathartic approach to anger means that the person relieves his or her emotion by expressing it. When Bill says he tried getting it off his chest when he was younger, he believed that it would make him feel better. Some counselors utilize this approach by having their counselees hit chairs with foam bats, scream at pictures, watch violent movies, or play aggressive sports. The assumption is that these activities will release some of the excess anger. But the question of whether or not catharsis works when it comes to resolving anger needs to be asked.

Three reviews of the experimental literature on catharsis raise serious questions around its viability. Berkowitz (1970) and Warren and Kurlychek (1981) reviewed over a dozen studies and found that people experience more anger and aggression, not less, when they witness or participate in aggressive behaviors. Lewis and Bucher (1992) drew similar conclusions and added that catharsis also runs the risk of people seeing themselves as helpless victims, thus preventing them from dealing with the anger in a helpful manner. These studies suggest that, at best, catharsis does not reduce anger and, at worst, it may even intensify it. The writer of the Proverbs may have been on to something when he said that a "fool gives full vent to his anger, but a wise man keeps himself under control" (29:11).

2

THE MASKS OF ANGER

Summary: In seeking an understanding of the individual's experience of anger, we begin by acknowledging that each person's experience is different. The commonality is in the experience of anger in its emotion and physiology. There are differences in the roots of anger that are explored in the breached goals, values, expectations, and sense of worth. Exploring the implosion and explosion of anger and the masking of its experiential, verbal, action, and spiritual ways may lead us to the unmasking of anger. The goal is to establish a productive cycle of anger, which is an accurate and appropriate expression of the person avoiding sinning against one's self, others, or God.

The Troublesome Emotion

Anger is a complex and confusing emotion, but much more than an emotion. This was clarified in the discussion of the myths of anger. Since our primary awareness of anger is as an emotion, let's start there. Anger is an emotion of displeasure, hurt, shame, pain, indignation, resentment, exasperation, or annoyance, all of which may range from mild to extreme. It manifests itself in criticizing, yelling, withdrawing, feelings of helplessness, shame, victimhood, scorn, scolding, ridiculing, humiliating, despising, teasing, putting down, or more physical activity such as hitting, hurting, damaging, attacking, or in other ways bringing harm to the focus of one's anger. With such a range of expression and outcomes, it is little wonder that we deny, cover, divert, displace, or seek to bury this troublesome emotion.

Anger: Experienced and Expressed

One may look at anger as an emotion that is *experienced* by the person, *expressed verbally* by the person, or *acted out* by the person. This threefold division is helpful in acknowledging the *person's experience,* the *person's verbal expression,* and the *person's actions* as three related but different dimensions. Often, it is helpful to initially look at the experience and expression of the person who is angry, rather than focusing on the outcomes for the recipients of the anger. When we focus on the recipient, we tend to induce guilt, which may inhibit understanding anger in the individual. It is helpful to overtly set aside the outcomes for the recipient through explicitly stating that intention. One might say, "Initially I would like you to focus on your experience of anger so that we may achieve an understanding of your experience. Later, we will look at the effect your anger has on others and what you wish to do about that, but for now let's understand your experience."

Anger Is Instrumental

Basic to this approach is the question: What does the anger accomplish for the person expressing it? Anger is often instrumental. A person may define it as reactive in that they perceive it as responsive to a stimulus provided by another, but it will normally have value to the person expressing it. It will be very helpful to achieve an understanding of what is accomplished by the person in their use of anger. Do they use it to intimidate, to get their own way, to avoid responsibility, or to motivate others in some way? The outcomes of anger specific to the person in the context of relationships may be very informative.

The Masks of Anger

We would like to look at the *masks of anger* as apparent in the person's *experience, verbal expression,* and *actions.* Taboos against the acknowledgment of and expression of anger are so strong in our culture that we have learned many ways to mask our experience so that neither we nor others are clearly aware of our anger. Masks develop because we perceive anger as threatening, irrational, and destructive, leading to rejection, disapproval, shame, or guilt. Masks confuse and, thereby, lead to the mismanagement of anger. Gentleness and artfulness must be exercised in unmasking anger. Helpers must be fully aware of the significance of the mask to the person. To aggressively or quickly seek to remove the mask may be experienced as abusive by the person and may lead to sufficient threat and termination of the relationship. With appropriate gentleness, one must bring the person to an awareness of the mask, its significance, and the desire to, in the safety of the counseling relationship, risk removal of the mask. Alternatives to masking must be explored and be seen as viable and safe before masks can be discarded and openness entered into as a mode of relating.

The *masks of anger* are mechanisms by which the person disguises, covers, or hides their anger. Often a mask will be entered into as a means of pretense by which the person implies the absence of anger, redirects the anger, diffuses the anger, or in some way distorts the real emotion. Masks may be used with intentionality or with a lack of consciousness. They frequently will have deep-seated roots in one's family of origin where they may have been learned. The person's personal or corporate safety may be sought through masking, or the person may function in this way to protect others from what is perceived by the person to be an uncontrollable and dangerous burst of energy and emotion. It is often helpful to differentiate between the energy, which we would define as the physiological aspects of anger, and the emotion, or the affective dimensions of anger as experienced by the person. One needs to bear in mind the discussion of Myth 4 in the first chapter. This will be expanded on later.

Anger: Fruit from a Family Tree

It is helpful to acknowledge that the fruit of anger grows in every family tree. An interesting and helpful study here is Jacob's family tree. One might explore the ways in which Jacob, Esau, and later the sons of Jacob expressed their anger. Jacob expressed his anger in relation to Esau and his parents and later in his relationship with Laban. Is there a relationship with the way his sons expressed their anger toward Joseph? One could make an interesting study of anger in a family by exploring the family of Jacob. The expression of anger has its roots in the soil of our family of origin. The fruit will vary in its manifestations. Anger may be described differently as it manifests itself in each family. The fruit of anger in a person's life will bear much resemblance to the fruit of anger produced and demonstrated in the family of origin.

The masks of anger are learned responses. It is helpful to lead people to a cataloguing of the way in which anger is/was masked in their family members and, then, in themselves. The compass direction that orients us in our expression of anger is significantly determined by our family of origin. The learning of the expression of anger occurs so young and so effectively that we operate on automatic pilot when anger is activated. The habitual expression learned becomes a reflex action that may be activated by triggers that provide the stimulus. The awareness of the triggers and origins of the patterns of action may be lost in the dim history of our youth. Part of the process of counseling will be to bring to awareness the experience of "automatic pilot" that is activated. When anger is expressed, whether expressed toward one's self or in relationship with others, it may be referred to as *anger investment*. When you deposit anger in a savings account you collect compound interest.

Anger: Implosion or Explosion?

Anger is experienced in several directions. Anger may *implode,* that is, it may *burst inward.* In this case, we are considering the effect on the person experiencing the anger. This manner of dealing with anger is often referred to as suppression, the keeping of the lid on it by consciously stuffing the feelings. Or it may involve repression, which is a case of burying the anger deeply in the unconscious and denying it. The implosion of anger will express itself in the physiological manifestation of anger in the body and may express itself in the feelings, actions, or spiritual abuse directed toward one's self.

Anger may *explode,* that is, it may *burst outward,* either being directed toward others, things, or God. Often this manner of dealing with anger is referred to as expression or letting it out by venting the emotions in temper or aggression. We prefer to focus on imploding and exploding first, and then consider the resultant impact of the expression on one's self, as well as others and the environment.

Experiential Masks of Anger

By experiential, we mean the person's experience of their anger. From this perspective, anger may be described as the *imploding, the bursting inward,* of the experience of anger upon the person experiencing it. This may be defined as the physiology of anger, the behavioral, emotional, relational, attitudinal, and spiritual outcomes of anger directed by the person toward the self. Anger may be masked in any of these areas. They dramatically impact the perception the individual has of self and, thus, will be determinative of the person's behavior toward others.

Often, the most nonthreatening place to start in counseling is to look at the *physiology of anger.* Most individuals will be much more aware of anger as an emotion than as a physiological reaction, but it is instructive to begin with the physiology. The physiology of anger is more basic than the emotions of anger, and more readily understood. To begin here will give a sense of understanding and accomplishment in the process of dealing with anger. It is instructive, as was noted in chapter 1, that Old Testament words for anger reflect bodily imagery. Anger is a physiological response activated by the autonomic nervous system, particularly the sympathetic part of the system, to ready or prepare us for action.

This physiological preparedness involves body chemistry, both in chemicals introduced directly into the blood, and chemicals (notably adrenaline) introduced into the stomach. Blood is redistributed throughout the body with large muscle systems becoming supercharged and the surface of the body being readily supplied to protect in the case of injury. Heart rate increases, lung function is enhanced, vascular changes are introduced, pupils become dilated, and many other changes prepare us for action. When one continues in this state of physiological arousal for lengthy periods of time, the stress placed on the body results in damage that may lead to physical pathology and the onset of psychosomatic symptoms. The symptoms evidenced will vary dramatically depending upon the health status of our different bodily systems, which are influenced by genetic factors. Thus resentment, bitterness, or prolonged or repetitive anger wears on the body and will express itself in disease.

The physical masks of anger bear much similarity to the physical manifestation of stress-induced disease. One must be careful to differentiate between physiological outcomes that are induced by stress, loss, trauma, and the like, and those that are an outcome of anger. Some of the more common physical masks, which may be indicators of an anger problem, include gastrointestinal complaints. Stomach sensitivity, ulcers, or related complaints may be anger related. Colitis and similar conditions may be correlated with the presence of anger. Low-grade infections may result from less than adequate functioning of the immune system, which may be impacted by discouragement or depression influenced by anger. It is common for people with anger problems to experience a variety of headaches, including migraine. Hypertension, in its various manifestations, may result from extended experiences of anger and the corollary presence of competitiveness, aggression, or the characteristics of a "Type A" personality. One should also be aware that vague viral-like symptoms, fatigue or chronic exhaustion, muscle or joint pain, and injuries from high-risk behavior may be related to anger mismanagement. One must exercise appropriate caution in assessing the physical masks of anger and have the necessary medical assessment of all of these conditions. It is extremely helpful to work in concert with a medical doctor in such an assessment. Each person will personalize the way in which anger may be masked in physical manifestations.

Being sensitive and assisting the individual to get in touch with the physical manifestations of anger may lead to the early identification of anger and the proper naming of it. The significance of naming anger in its physical dimensions is vitally important in that naming something often is a big step toward exercising control and mastery in dealing with it effectively. Anger imploded leads one to become one's own worst enemy. There are many ways for this to express itself, other than in the physiology indicated above.

Behaviorally, one may act toward one's self with aggression or malice. This may express itself in high-risk behavior, which leads to accidents and pain, entering into abusive relationships where one will become the victim, the use of harmful substances, withdrawal from nurturing relationships or opportunities, or the demonstrating of objectionable behavior that will lead to rejection or punishment.

One may engage in *emotional* blackmail against one's self by emotional distancing, fantasy, daydreaming, sadness or depression, or any form of regression. When one sees these present, one should be open to ask if they arise from anger being directed inward.

Relationally, one may evidence imploding anger in isolating or overbonding, the sabotaging of relationships for personal pain, rebellion or immoral behavior that is motivated by the pursuit of punishment, selective inattention that leads to conflict in relationships, or the entering into conflict to effect rejection. When one sees a person submitting in extreme ways, one should explore anger toward self issues.

Most frequently, *attitudinal* implosion expresses itself in condemning oneself, a constant focus on one's inadequacies, or a tragic sense of life that expresses itself in self-induced shame or despair.

Spiritual self-abuse will demonstrate itself in legalism, rigidity, an unforgiving attitude toward self, a subjugation of self to cult leadership, a focus on spiritual failure, and interpretation of abandonment by God. It may express itself in a "worm theology" or a death-to-self focus in one's thinking. This may manifest in false humility which is self-depreciating, or in claims of worthlessness which fail to acknowledge the efficacy of God's grace and the value of the person as a residence of the Spirit of God and his giftedness.

Again, it is important to point out that we are not suggesting the presence of these are always indications of imploding anger. However, one would do well to explore the person's direction of anger toward self in understanding whether any of the above are in fact masks of anger. If so, dealing with the mask and getting behind the mask to the real issue of anger, and treating anger as the issue rather than focusing on the mask may prove helpful.

Anger: Verbal Masks

Being the cognitive persons we are, it is not surprising that one of the most common ways we mask anger is with our verbal behavior. Again, it is helpful to ask: What is accomplished by this person by the verbal behavior they are expressing?

Verbal masks of anger may be of the implosion or explosion variety. The face of anger may be masked by a great variety of verbal gymnastics. Again, anger is going underground. Verbal implosion will usually evidence anger being covered by directing attention toward one's self to elicit sympathy, attention, or aggression in such a way as to cover the anger with a facade that obfuscates any anger. *Verbal implosion* is often expressed in self-negation. One may be seeking to deflect attention by disappearing behind a mask of self-abuse. This may have the effect of eliciting sympathy for my self-declared victimhood or attracting aggression or abuse of one so guilty or shameful.

Just today a husband expressed his insight about himself regarding this tactic. "I so frequently in response to my wife's anger make myself a victim of myself. I don't like her anger. So, I put myself down in an attempt to change her anger into sympathy. I guess I think she wouldn't hit a man when he is down." This may be expressed by "playing dead," such as we are told is sometimes effective when being attacked by a grizzly bear. If I become passive by turning my anger inward, I can mask it rather than express it. Or, I may be more active in verbally putting myself down. It is safer to beat myself than to express my anger toward others and, besides, they may be sympathetic and kind if I beat myself. This person may be a *passive pessimist* who retreats into silence or self-blame as a means of masking anger.

Verbal explosion may take many forms, including the following. The *verbal bully* may bite and cut using "bitter speech as an arrow" (Ps. 64:3), or be "one who speaks rashly like thrusts of a sword" (Ps. 57:4; Prov. 12:18), or who "crush(es) me with words" (Job 19:2) exercising "the scourge of the tongue" (Job 5:21). Such verbal aggression may mask anger, which would be more manageable if dealt with overtly. The wise man said, "Death and life are in the power of the tongue" (Prov. 18:21 NASB). Relational death occurs when anger is masked by the verbal bully. Related to the verbal bully is the person who uses *poisonous parlay* to frighten others away or into submission.

Meaningless messages are expressed in a verbal dance that dazzles as the person trips around issues by dealing with everything trivial and thus avoids the substance of anger. In response to another's expression of anger, some persons will introduce much unrelated trivia as a diversional tactic. *Compulsive conversationalists,* likewise, overwhelm with breathless verbiage to subvert meaningful addressing of anger. A cousin of the compulsive conversationalist is the *talk, talk* person who through excessive explanation overwhelms with quantity of verbiage that is so, so rational.

Sneak speakers sabotage indirectly through divisive tactics that baffle and confuse issues. The *silent signalers* communicate with nonverbal sighs, sniffs, snorts, or other such masks of discontent. The opposite of these are the *loud language* communicators who frighten the quiet with decibels of noise. More subtle are the *but blurbs* who give the appearance of niceness with their sincere, "I like you, but . . ." twist of the knife. The *truth tellers* also profess compassion insisting that they speak in love, but their message is one of rigidity, legalism, and exaggeration presented under the guise of truth. Thus the truth teller covers anger with the hypocritical mask of love and concern. Perhaps, most nauseating are the *sweet signalers* who sweet talk you into drowning in their syrup or liquid honey. The number of ways to mask anger with verbal expression are legion, including sarcasm, selective inattention, or many other mutations.

Anger: Action Masks

Much fear is generated in response to the behavioral expression of anger. Most of us have had rather bad ineffectual outcomes in our lives and relationships as a result of our expression of anger. In this sense, the problem is not anger, but the expression of an aroused state of physical energy and preparedness. It is very helpful to clearly distinguish between anger and its expression. The experience of anger is a natural response determined by our humanity, and, as we have already seen, a dimension of the reality of being created in the image and likeness of God. The expression of anger is learned in its verbal, action, and spiritual manifestations. It seems that we experience more fear in response to the learned actions we enter into as we experience anger than we do in relation to either the verbal or spiritual expressions. However, the verbal and spiritual are often extremely harmful whether they are expressed in implosion or explosion.

The *drama of anger* is acted out toward ourselves, others, and God, but also significantly toward our environment. There may be much confused mixing of these actions in that they may affect self, others, God, and our environment all at the same time. In counseling, we often see one bringing harm to one's self through substance abuse, physical harm (such as cutting one's self), or in accidents. These behaviors may at the same time dramatically affect others, harm the environment, be a "shaking of one's fist in the face of God," or challenge God to demonstrate love in rescuing. Satan tempted Christ to leap from the temple, having the assurance that God would let no harm come to him. This would not have been an act of anger on the part of Christ. However, sometimes people will, in anger, challenge the care of God or the care of others in a foolish attempt to elicit sympathy, love, or attention.

It is very important to assess the effects of behavior expressed in anger. People are often willing to look at the effect of their behavior on others from the perspective of harm to them. This may be encouraged by the legal ramifications or by the most obvious damage to the other person. It may be more difficult for one to see that the behavior of anger may be motivated by the benefit that comes to the one expressing the anger.

Anger is not only learned, but it is also purposeful and may be overtly or covertly intentional. Carefully analyzing the drama of anger specific to the individual may help to differentiate between anger and its expression, and at the same time enables one to access the purpose, whether that is power, control, punishment of self or others, or other outcomes that are desired.

It may be helpful to understand that anger is a reflex action involving emotions and physiology. The expression of anger is a secondary response, learned and purposeful, which can be unlearned and for which more effective means can be learned to accomplish acceptable goals to which we are committed. In identifying the desired outcomes of anger, we create the possibility of evaluating those outcomes in terms of our values and commitments.

An example of the problem that can arise when we fail to distinguish between anger and its expression may be provided by looking at anger and aggression. Anger and aggression are not the same. Anger is an emotional and physiological response. Aggression is a behavioral acting out verbally with bitter speech, or violent actions that often contain an element of meanness that is invariably destructive, or an attempt to be destructive to another. It confuses our understanding of anger to include aggression in its definition.

It is important to assess whether the actions of anger are directed toward people or things. It is not uncommon for persons to give themselves permission to destroy property or to attack their environment, but not to give themselves permission to harm people directly. In working with delinquents, we discovered that it was important to know if they, in expressing anger, were likely to break furniture or attack supervisors. Some would enter into action that clearly resulted in the possibility of personal harm, but would control themselves in their actions toward other persons. In counseling, it is often helpful to uncover the power of choice, which is invariably made in the selection of the means of expressing or the object of one's anger. People are often surprised to discover the choices they make. Strengthening that power of choice may be very important.

Some always direct their anger personward. An illustration of this was the man whose wife accused him of "wood swearing." He habitually, when angry, slammed doors throughout the house and broke furniture, but would never raise his voice in cursing or touch his wife or children. In fact, he exercised considerable choice and control in his expression of anger. A point to understand here is that people have the capacity of control, but it is selective control and learned behavior that has been defined as acceptable. In counseling, we would focus on the ability of the person to control and work toward the extension of that control through developing more effective means of expressing anger in action.

The drama of anger may be acted out in habitual lateness, selective inattention, physical posturing, gestures of control or threat, aggressive behaviors, physical withdrawal, or many other actions that are learned and often become reflexive. The actions that mask anger must be clearly catalogued and will be peculiar to the individual. The artistry of the counselor will be evident in assisting the counselee to objectively stand back and watch the drama of anger that is expressed in the actions with which he/she expresses anger. The achievement of self-understanding and some degree of objectivity as one stands outside one's self as an observer is foundational to dealing with anger.

Anger: Spiritual Masks

Perhaps the most difficult masks of anger to deal with are the spiritual masks of anger. When a person resorts to spiritualizing their expression of anger, they often are unconscious of doing so and quite resistant to identifying the process. There will frequently be an overlay of religious justification or an elevation of their anger response to what they may describe as righteous indignation. The provocation to anger will often be exaggerated or absolutized in terms of evil so that it demands the response of indignation. On the other hand, the values being represented by the angry person will also be absolutized so that to appear to address it or object to it is tantamount to objecting to God-ordained values. Perhaps it is a case of the person who feels so good to hate evil so greatly. After all, one surely is justified in taking the side of God! Are attacks on people who believe differently sometimes a covert expression of anger with a spiritual overlay? Often, we fear the debates that rage among Christians who accusatively belittle, berate, and blatantly condemn one another are an expression of unadulterated anger rather than an expression of spiritual passion. Or, perhaps, it is just an attempt to bolster a weak argument by creating a cloud of noxious smoke to throw off the person with the better argument. Whatever the case, anger wears spiritual masks.

One may justify legalism, rigidity, criticism, aggression, or attacking the perpetrator of evil as a cover or mask for one's personal anger. Great wisdom is needed in discerning when such expressions are motivated by anger that is energized by personal gain or advantage rather than by the appropriate pursuit of values. Persons who cover their anger with spiritual masks are energized by caustic, "fire-topped," rather than copper-topped batteries. Often the question as to the personal gain for the person may lead to understanding the degree to which such action is creating a spiritual mask for one's anger.

Sometimes, it appears to us that a spiritual mask evidencing implosion of anger may express itself in a spiritual negation in which one devalues one's self and professes abandonment by God, spiritual bankruptcy, or a negation of one's giftedness. It may be possible that "the devil made me do it" attitude is an abdication of responsibility and an expression of anger at one's lack of control or discipline. Another form of this may be the person who does evil as a test of the love of another in a "can you love me when I'm this bad?" experiment.

It appears sometimes that what people describe as "expressing the truth in love" may in fact be a spiritual masking of anger. In such a way, one can justify some very harsh and unloving comments that may express anger. Often the evidence will be that there is a much stronger focus on "truth expression" than on the process being characterized by love.

The frequent role of spiritual masks of anger to provide self-justification makes it difficult to deal with these masks and, for this reason, the counselor's acute awareness of them is essential to getting behind the masks. Spiritual masking of anger may be closely related to the traditional understanding of repression and the accompanying resistance to change. Spiritual masks may be very difficult to confront and equally difficult to give up because of the vulnerability to responsibility that accompanies the loss of a mask justified by God, in the mind of the person.

Anger as a Mask

Anger itself may be a mask. It may be that individuals have learned only the expression of anger and it becomes a cover for other more tender emotions they have not learned to own and express. It may cover other hurts which, being unhealed, cannot be exposed. For example, Jeff used anger as a mask to cover tender feelings which he did not learn to express as a child. Not experiencing the level of affection and nurture that he desired, either eliciting from him or being expressed to him, he masked those emotions with anger which seemed to justify his experience. It may cover many other motivations, such as desire for recognition, control, power, desire for attention or care, and so on.

When anger itself is discovered to be a mask for other emotions, it is dealt with as a secondary emotion and the focus may shift to understanding what is being covered. In that case, one must focus on exploring, understanding, and developing strategies for expressing the masked emotion. It is important to be open to considering whether anger is a mask, or if it is being masked.

Unmasking Anger

The central message of this book is that we must name and own anger and assume responsibility for the appropriate and effective expression of it. Without leaping ahead to issues of the process of counseling, we would like to make a couple of observations at this point. To repeat what was said at the beginning of this chapter, masks are usually protective devices learned and used to protect from threat or perceived danger. They confuse both the person experiencing the anger and others involved or observing. It is not helpful to use the discussion of masks as a means of generating guilt or shame. Masks may be very important to the person. The goal is to explore and understand the masks as an avenue to understanding the person's experience of anger and expression of anger.

Only when these are understood and alternative strategies are in place will the person be likely to be open to dropping the mask. As indicated earlier, one must create a safe environment in which a person can explore and achieve understanding of their masks and achieve a degree of objectivity. This is aided by acknowledging and affirming with genuineness the degree of selectivity and choice that is made in expressing one's anger. The person may be led from a place of powerlessness in the face of anger to an acknowledgment that they do, in fact, make choices and, thus, have some potential for control. Focusing on the healthy and appropriate choices a person makes may engender a sense of competence and power for change that will not come with a focus on the pathology in the person's behavior. The work of David Waters and Edith Lawrence (1991) is helpful in presenting this "non-pathological" perspective.

Gentleness and artfulness must be exercised in unmasking anger. A helpful way to access the masks of anger may be to look at the *imagery of anger*. Frequently, the imagery used to explicate one's anger is very informative. One may say, "He turns my stomach," "I was blind with anger," "She smothers me," or "I felt like I would burst." The imagery may reflect the mask that will be used to cover the anger. For example, one woman masked her anger with nausea and vomiting and spoke of the behavior of another who angered her as "turning her stomach." Another may mask anger with migraines or headaches, another with asthma or hypertension. We would observe that there sometimes appears to be a correlation between the mask and the imagery used to express the sensation or experience. It is useful to encourage people to express their anger in imagery.

Cynthia spoke of her anger as her being placed in a box by a rather controlling husband. She defined "being boxed" as something her husband did to her. However, in exploring this, she discovered that there is both an inside and outside to the box. In truth, she experienced much comfort being in the box because it became self-protection from her personal expression of anger. Inside the box, she was safe from expressing the anger she feared so much. She was able to own her part in her own "boxing" when she owned her anger and developed appropriate expression for it. Working with the person's imagery, and, indeed, helping them to create imagery that represents and explicates their experience, provides much understanding and insight.

The Equation of Anger

Anger is unmasked through the process of accepting, exploring, understanding, and owning anger and the assumption of responsibility for the appropriate expressing of anger with honesty and integrity. As implied already, we feel this is best accomplished by differentiating between the expression of anger, which most of us have come to fear, and our experience of anger as emotion and physiological arousal, which prepares us for action. Another dimension to the equation of anger is to achieve an understanding of what elicits or provokes this response in us. What generates or fuels this activation process which leads us to an aroused, prepared state for action? Let's forget for a moment the issues related to expression. That is important, but needs to be put into abeyance so that we do not get caught up in or rendered impotent by the guilt or shame that may be induced by focusing on the effect of our expression of anger.

If we go behind the emotion and physiological dimensions of anger, we discover that four elements are present, either singly or in concert with each other. First, when I experience a *breach of my goals,* I respond with anger. Goals may arise from a variety of sources. They become personalized and owned by each person. When these goals are thwarted or blocked in some way, I respond with anger. The anger will be directed at the person or object that is blocking the realization of the goal, if I feel safe in expressing anger in that direction. However, if I do not feel safe, I may choose to displace my anger in some way that appears safer to me. Or, on the other hand, I may implode my anger.

Second, anger is elicited when we experience a *breach of values.* When our values are breached, we experience a surge of anger. Interestingly, it would appear from many biblical illustrations that God experiences anger when his values are breached. If one has experienced much injustice in childhood, justice may become a significant commitment and have great importance to an individual. When that value is breached, the person will experience a surge of emotion and physical preparedness which energizes one to defend the value. Similarly, if the value of friendship, trust, care for one another, honesty, or any of many other values is breached, we react with anger. It is interesting to note that we each hold different values with different degrees of commitment and react with greater passion when our personal values are breached. Our expression in emotion and behavior to a breach of values may range from withdrawal to aggressive acting out, from indignation to passive victimhood, or any other avenue of expression.

But let's not get into expression. It is such a temptation to try to stop or change the outcome of anger. Stay with the issue of breached values. An appropriate question to explore may be put this way: How well do my values reflect God's values? The answer may lead to an affirmation of the value, a clarifying of the value, or a change of the value. It will become patently clear that my behavior does not well represent or appropriately reflect the value. However, we are at this point in a position to inform the expression of our anger with our commitment to the value which was breached in the arousal of the anger. This is a significant step from reflexively expressing myself in ways that bear no relationship to the value which was breached. One of the outcomes of counseling will be the development of new behaviors that truly and honestly represent my values, using the energy of anger to do this well. These issues will be elaborated in a counseling session in a later chapter.

Third, anger is elicited when we experience a *breach of expectations*. It may be my expectation to be accepted, loved, to have dinner ready when I come home, to never be late or kept waiting, to be greeted at a party, to be given the right of way on the highway, and so on. When my expectations are breached, I experience anger. The breach of expectations may generate a sense of rejection, a fear of loss, distrust, jealousy, a loss of significance, or any of a whole range of emotions. Exploring with the counselee the catalogue of expectations that they bring to the context in which anger is experienced is very helpful in clarifying what, in fact, is initiating the anger they are experiencing. Exploring the source or appropriateness of my expectations and the owning of them may lead to more effective ways of expressing those expectations. If I can name, own, and find appropriate ways to discuss my expectations and to let them be known, I will be more effective in correcting them or having them met. This, too, will be illustrated in the counseling sessions.

Fourth, when I experience a *breach of my sense of worth*, I respond with anger. If my ego is damaged or bruised by criticism, a verbal thrust of another's sword, a devaluation of my self, or any other form of put-down, it is not unusual for me to respond with anger. Obviously, the strength of my ego and the communal network wherein I experience significance, my assurance of acceptance by God, and many other variables will determine how sensitive I am to a breach of my sense of worth. However, if I know that my anger is evoked by a breach of my sense of worth, I may be directed to work on the issue of my sense of worth and wherein it resides. Dealing with that issue may significantly impact my experience of anger. However, if I clarify that that is the thing eliciting my anger, I may be able to deal with that in relation to the person who has breached my self-worth, rather than simply exploding toward the person in anger. Again, this will be illustrated in the counseling sessions.

Understanding the anger equation may be very helpful in unmasking anger and getting behind the anger to the issues that need to be addressed. In fact, exploring the goals, values, expectations, and self-worth, and their being breached will be much more effective than focusing on either the anger itself or its manifestation as expressed by the person. This is getting at the experience of the person at a level they may have little or no awareness of, but which may enable the addressing of foundational issues and thereby effect change.

Defining Anger

To this point, we have not attempted to define anger. Obviously, there are clear implications in what we have written to imply a definition. The expressive dimensions of behavior do not adequately define anger, but only its outcomes. The source from which anger springs, that is, breached goals, values, expectations, our sense of worth, does not define anger. Anger is that middle part of the equation, which may be defined as emotional and physiological preparedness for action and may have many motivations and many means of expressing itself. If we take the biblical injunction "Be angry and sin not" seriously, we must recognize that anger is not the essential problem. It is possible to be angry and not sin. Sin may manifest itself in our goals, values, expectations, or sense of worth. On the other hand, sin may manifest itself in our expression of our anger whether learned in our family, acquired along the way, or as a result of our own imaginative propensity to sin.

A simple working definition of anger will provide us with a place to start in our understanding of the experience: Anger is an experience that occurs when a goal, value, or expectation that I have chosen has been blocked or when my sense of personal worth is threatened. This experience involves emotions, physiology, and cognitive processes and expresses itself toward self, others, or the environment.

PERSONAL FACTORS	EXPERIENCE	EXPRESSION
blocking of goals	emotions	imploding
breach of values	thoughts	exploding > others
breach of expectations breach of sense of worth }	physiology	God, things > hurt

In the following charts we illustrate a nonproductive and productive cycle of anger.

An Illustration of Nonproductive and Productive Cycles of Anger

A Nonproductive Anger Cycle

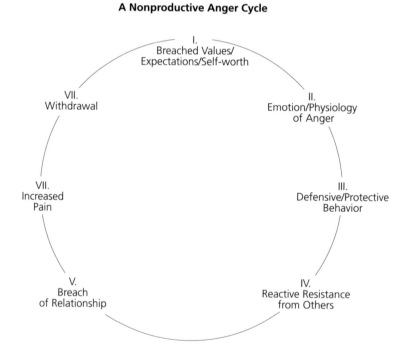

A Productive Anger Cycle

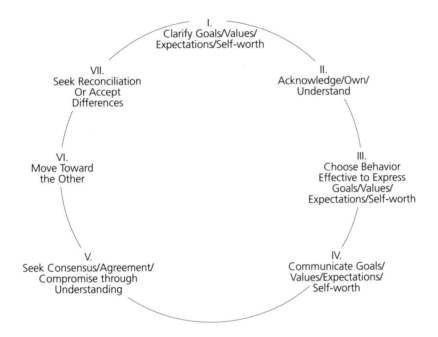

I.
Clarify Goals/Values/
Expectations/Self-worth

II.
Acknowledge/Own/
Understand

III.
Choose Behavior
Effective to Express
Goals/Values/
Expectations/Self-worth

IV.
Communicate Goals/
Values/Expectations/
Self-worth

V.
Seek Consensus/Agreement/
Compromise through
Understanding

VI.
Move Toward
the Other

VII.
Seek Reconciliation
Or Accept
Differences

3

EXASPERATION AND ANGER
SESSION 1

Summary: Session 1 has four particular goals. In joining and boundary setting, the pastor seeks to make contact with the couple and
establish parameters for what will follow. The second goal is to
explore the key concerns and determine the relevant history. The
pastor then moves to the process of conducting a pastoral diagnosis so there is some specificity as to the nature of the problem.
Finally, the pastor and the couple seek to develop a mutually
acceptable focus for the counseling.

Clarifying the Purpose of Session 1

As a pastoral counselor anticipates Session 1, it is important to
clearly have in mind what you wish to accomplish and the process
by which you will do this. It is helpful to distinguish between outcome goals and process goals. The broad outcome desired is to

encounter the person(s) in establishing the personal contact which provides the context for counseling. It is helpful to understand that the relationship in counseling is different than the relationship for preaching/teaching, hospital care, social relationships, or the many other encounters the pastor may have with the parishioner who comes for counseling. Confusing these roles inevitably reduces effectiveness in ministry. The four outcome goals may be expressed as

joining and boundary setting;
exploring the central concerns and relevant history;
conducting a pastoral diagnosis;
achieving a mutually agreeable focus for counseling.

In this chapter, we would like to provide some excerpts from the first counseling session with Bill and Joy and then elaborate some of the process goals that were in mind as we sought to achieve the outcomes desired in a first session.

In the counseling sessions, we desire to communicate a level of acceptance, which will provide a safe context for the counselees to explore and to learn. It is helpful to distinguish between acceptance and approval or condoning. This has often been expressed as unconditional positive regard. Pastors may have to think through that issue carefully if they have a strong sense of a prophetic role or the role of a culture carrier in the community of faith they represent. When pastors enter the counseling relationship, they must consider whether their congregation perceives them to be "gatekeepers" or persons who are to at all times represent the ideals of the congregation. Does accepting a person who has fallen short of the ideals of the Christian life mean that we are being easy on sin or not holding forth the truth clearly enough? Will we be criticized for not confronting sin? Will the counseled person mistake acceptance for approval? If any of these questions are relevant for the pastor, he may need to carefully clarify these for himself and for the counselees.

We must clarify the distinctives of Strategic Pastoral Counseling with its emphases upon brevity, scriptural focus, wholistic nature, and structural framework. A pastor's training may have exposed him to counseling that is characterized by a client-centered, cognitive, behavioristic, or psychoanalytical approach. It will be very helpful to clearly keep in mind the distinctives of Strategic Pastoral Counseling and to clarify any ambiguity that may exist in the minds of the counselees. Clarifying the expectations of the counselees may be very important.

The quality of the pastoring, shepherding relationship will inform the process goals of counseling. These may be expressed by such biblical concepts as strengthening (Acts 14:22; 15:32, 41; 16:5), care (Acts 16:3), building up (Acts 9:31; 20:2), exhorting (Acts 11:23; 14:22; 15:32; 20:2), persuading (Acts 11:23; 13:43), comforting (Acts 9:31), or admonishing (Acts 20:20–32). These are only some of the process words that described the nurturing ministry in the Acts of the Apostles. The Epistles are replete with such instruction. We would define edification as being to another person what that person needs you to be for their good and resultant growth (Rom. 15:1). Comfort is coming alongside another to bear his/her need, that they might be encouraged and strengthened. Confronting might be defined as kindly but firmly bringing one another to the awareness of discrepancies or incongruity between our lives and the will of God. The ministry of Christ richly informs the process of counseling as he cared for people.

Adult Learning and Homework

The expectations and reasons for both the emphasis on the ownership of the counselees in the process of counseling and the assignment of homework are based on the assumptions of adult education. Persons grow and mature as they move from dependency to increasing self-directedness, which is in many ways mediated by one's self-concept and the expectations of others. People enter into new learning as they are encouraged to identify resources within themselves to see past experience as a reservoir for learning through experimentation. Readiness to learn is influenced by imbedding learning in the desire for change in social roles. Learning will be entered into more readily if learning is associated with problem solving in response to a sense of inadequacy in specific situations. Resources for understanding these principles may be found in two classic books by Malcolm Knowles (1973) and Carl Rogers (1969). These principles can be incorporated both into counseling and into the assignment of homework.

In assigning homework, it is important to evidence its relevance in the ensuing sessions and to move from the understanding achieved to its application in the real life situation being addressed. Some of the benefits that come from assigning homework would be the following: it saves time; takes pressure off pastor and parishioner in the counseling situation; is a way to assess motivation; extends the length of the session; reinforces material discussed in the session; sets up issues to be discussed in the next session; and communicates that counseling is a shared responsibility. Homework may involve different types of interaction, such as specific directions to think about something; specific directions to do something; open-ended assignments capitalizing on the strengths of the person (i.e. music, poetry, and the like); a sentence completion device that fits their particular problem; or a writing assignment that lets them see what they are feeling/thinking/acting in a given situation.

Note Taking

Counselors differ in their practice of note taking. Some find it too obtrusive and distracting to take notes in the sessions. This is probably a question of the way in which one has learned to listen and one's style of attending to another person. If note taking in the session is distracting for the counselor, it is probably distracting for the counselee as well. This has much to do with the ability of the counselor to carefully attend to the counselee and at the same time to take notes. Some are much more effective if the focus is on one thing at a time. The conclusion, then, would be to determine the effect of note taking on one's self, and to assess the effect of note taking on the counselee(s) and to adjust accordingly.

If one can cope with the division of attention between the coun-selee(s) and one's notes, then it is likely to be very helpful. This may be more important in the structured counseling model being proposed inasmuch as it places considerable responsibility on the counselor to be directive and to orchestrate the sessions toward the agreed upon goals. Thus you may wish to remember details that will not be addressed immediately because of the distraction introduced, but you may wish to note the issue so that it will not be lost and can be returned to later.

Above all, note taking should be nonobtrusive to the relation-ship. Brevity, short forms, or, if one wishes, some form of short-hand may be helpful. It is not appropriate to make note taking a covert exercise. It is often wise to overtly explain the reason for note taking and to inquire if it is distracting to the persons involved. If it is presented as one more way to make the coun-seling experience more effective, most would agree to its use.

It is also wise to review one's notes immediately following the session. The purpose of this will be to provide an opportunity for reflection while the affective content of the session is still in one's awareness. It will be opportune at this time to add additional observations, make clarifications, expand the material, develop hypotheses to be later tested and clarified, and to formulate a plan as to the most appropriate direction or focus to bring to the next session. The busy life of a pastor requires such a methodology of keeping track of details that will otherwise be lost in the intensity of other demands between sessions.

Personally, we find having a notepad that can be used to illus-trate graphically some of the issues or dynamics being addressed adds greatly to the process. Sometimes a visual presentation of what is transpiring may communicate more effectively than words alone. Often developing a diagrammatic representation of what is evolving in the session is a much more effective teaching tool than a preprinted drawing, which may feel like an imposition on the experience of the people involved. There is something more personal about an illustration that is created in response to the immediate material presented. It is always important to consider the impact of note taking in each different situation.

Background to the First Session

Following the series "Anger: Mine and Yours" which Bill and Joy attended faithfully, Bill approached Pastor Harvey and they agreed to meet for counseling together with Joy. A time for the first session was agreed upon. However, on the appointed evening a hospital emergency required Pastor Harvey's attention and he arrived at the church office fifteen minutes late for the appointment. Although he had phoned to inform the church secretary and Bill and Joy of his lateness, he was also aware that this may be an opportunity for him to observe their response to an experience of being kept waiting.

Upon entering the reception area, Bill was observed to be pacing the floor, scowling, shoulders drooped, hands stuffed in his pockets, evidencing frustration and exasperation. Joy was sitting, appearing passive, but wearing a sweet smile while evidently trying to avoid seeing or acknowledging Bill's discontent.

> *Pastor:* Sorry to be late. Mr. Berry was rushed to the hospital with a heart attack. I was called and did not know how serious things were and the traffic was the pits. Let's go into my office. I'll catch my breath and we'll get started.
> *Bill does not respond overtly. Both Bill and Joy move toward office.*
> *Joy:* That's OK. I hope Mr. Berry recovers well.
> *Pastor Harvey offers chair to Joy and Bill. Bill slumps into the chair. Joy sits sedately with a broad smile, evidently ignoring Bill. The pastor sits in a chair facing both somewhat indirectly.*

Joining and Boundary Setting

> *Pastor:* Bill and Joy, I need to tell you that I appreciated your faithfulness in attending the series we recently concluded. In fact, you have both been an encouragement to me and others in the church. Sunday school teaching, your involvement in hockey with the youth, Bill, and yours with the Pioneer Club, Joy, have made you valued and contributing members. You both are appreciated.

Joy beams. Bill looks with questioning appreciation and appears somewhat relieved.

Bill: Thanks. I've benefited from my involvement in the past few years.

Pastor: Bill, before the series on anger, you and I had a brief conversation about your experience with anger. I appreciated your openness and desire to explore this more. And, Joy, I am glad you want to be a part of this. Let me clarify a couple of things so we all know what to expect. Normally, I find a one-hour session to be about maximum at one time, and, since I was late, we'll still have all of the hour we need. Since we have much contact outside these sessions and are part of the same church family, it is important to raise the question of confidentiality. I want you to know that nothing we talk about in these sessions will leave this office. If I feel that it is important for me to share something from our session outside the office, I will talk with you first. I don't know why that would happen, but if I believe it is important I will discuss it with you. Anything I share with you about myself, I'd appreciate being treated in the same way. We will reserve our discussion of issues or concerns raised here to being dealt with when we are in the counseling sessions. We don't want our relationships in other parts of our church life and ministry to be interfered with by what we discuss here. Does this seem appropriate and acceptable to you?

Bill: Yeah, I'd feel better knowing that. Does that mean Joy and I shouldn't discuss at home or with others what we talk about here?

Pastor: Do you have some sense as to the best way to handle that or what the effect might be, Bill?

Bill: Well, sometimes we don't do so good in discussing issues and *(pause)* Joy sometimes likes to talk to her sister.

Joy: I only talk to her when I'm hurt, or have no one else to talk to.

Pastor: Well, you both expressed important concerns. Sometimes we have trouble discussing "hot" issues but we do like to be heard when we hurt. We have to come back to these. Let's agree for now that we'll reserve our counseling time for discussing these issues and we'll try to provide an opportunity here to share our hurts. We need to move on to identify what we specifically want to deal with in these times together.

The pastor, upon entering the reception area, made a mental note of the nonverbal expressions present. He chose not to focus on them because it would have distracted from the purpose of the first session. It will, however, provide some basis for hypotheses concerning Bill's expression of anger, frustration, and so on or it may be indicative of his anxiety about being there. We can hardly emphasize enough the importance of the pastor assuming the responsibility of determining what is most profitable to focus on and the sequence with which issues will be raised and dealt with at any given time. We are not seeking to be simply responsive and to be led where the counseled wishes to go, but must stay focused on the issue at hand. The temptation to go off on many possible tracks is always present in encountering people on their adventure of life's journey. For example, Joy's presentation of herself may suggest a passivity, avoidance in acknowledging Bill's discomfort, or a mask of sweetness that may cover anger. Awareness of these clues is important. It would be very easy at this point to jump in to address or clarify the potential issues inherent in this observation. However, equally important is the selectivity exercised in deciding what to focus on and in what sequence to do so. One role of the counselor is the orchestration of the counseling sessions toward the goals mutually agreed on. Keen observation will provide much data that can be used in developing hypotheses, but the selective introduction or exploration of issues is part of the art of the helping relationship.

The first two comments of the pastor are specifically intended to effect joining, reduce tension, encourage comfort, and establish rapport. The affirmation in this comment is intended to acknowledge their maturity, wellness, competence, and to communicate respect. There is evidence that much value comes from identifying health as well as pathology in counselees. It provides a sense of one's ability to change, to grow, to assume responsibility, and acknowledges the mastery they have achieved in other areas of their lives. A good example of this emphasis is Waters and Lawrence (1991) who apply these principles in family therapy. Genuine respect for areas of competence builds a foundation for the partnership that is involved in counseling. It is important to recognize that some of the counseling methods used in dealing with deeper psychological or psychiatric issues are not appropriate when applied to pastoral counseling. The biblical imagery of the helping or caring relationship evidences much more the characteristics of a partnership than of a professional or clinical relationship.

The purpose of the pastor's third response is intended to begin to establish boundaries by addressing an awareness of confidentiality, length of sessions, and differentiating between the way we function and what we discuss in the sessions and our relationship in the church community outside of the sessions. One of the anxieties that may be brought to the sessions is the question of the impact of counseling on relationships outside the sessions. This is an issue that is more important to address for the pastor who will have other contexts in which to relate than for the professional counselor who is unlikely to see the counseled between sessions. The comfort of the counselee will be greatly enhanced if he or she has a clear understanding of the *boundaries,* the expectations, and the care that will be exercised to prevent the occurrences in the sessions from adversely affecting the relationship outside the sessions. Moving from the pastoring/teaching role into the counseling role and back again is something a pastor needs to think about deeply. This is important for his own well-being, as well as for the parishioner.

Bill raises another important issue of how the counseling should impact or be influenced by their relationship outside the counseling session and how it should be dealt with in sharing with others. The question of boundaries is not only important between the pastor and the counselee, but also between the counselee and other people in his/her life. Personally, we feel there is not a general rule to apply here. It depends on the nature of the problem and whether the couple has a process of communication that will permit discussion without deepening the problem. Sometimes it is appropriate to encourage a moratorium on discussion concerning certain issues outside the counseling session until a greater or more accurate understanding of the problem is achieved. It is important to reduce the amount of bruising that couples may inflict on each other between sessions. Reducing the invalidating responses they experience between each other greatly increases the prospects of seeing improvement in the relationship and of moving the relationship to more effective levels of functioning. Bill's next comment suggests he may be concerned about Joy talking to others, especially her sister. A note of this should be made as a possible issue to be addressed later.

The pastor's next comment is an attempt to honor Bill and to imply that the counseled is often looked to for the answer to their own question. This, additionally, has the impact of reducing the likelihood that the pastor will be cast in the role of the expert who is expected to give all the answers. It is important early in the relationship to establish expectations of the participative role of the counseled. Requesting their analysis, suggestions, observations, and the like is an appropriate way to help them to accept responsibility for what happens in the counseling and its outcomes. This also communicates a respect and carries the implication that they, in fact, have much to bring to the therapeutic process. They are not there to have something done to them, but rather bring their resources along with those of the pastor to apply to their area of difficulty.

Joy's response to Bill's comment referring to her sister may be very loaded, indicating the way she defines her anger and her feeling, and the interpretation that Bill is not there for her to talk with. The pastor chooses not to get caught up in any of the potential issues raised by either Bill or Joy at this point. However, in acknowledging the depth of feeling, he is not minimizing their comments. The decision is not to ignore the comments, but having noted them he decides that to focus on the issues raised would be counterproductive at this point, as joining and boundary setting are the immediate goals. He alternatively chooses to give positive reinforcement to their expressions by valuing both comments, indicating they will be dealt with later, and sets the stage to move to the next phase of the session, which is to deal with exploring the central concerns and relevant history.

Exploring and Identifying Central Concerns and Relevant History

Pastor: Let's tonight, in the time remaining, see if we can identify and clarify what would be most helpful to focus on in our time together over the next few weeks. Bill, you initially indicated a willingness and commitment to explore the area of anger and indicated it was a problem for both you and Joy. I assume you still wish to grow in your understanding of that area. Is that a fair assumption?

Bill: Yes, although I did get some help in understanding anger from the series. Yet, I don't always know how that fits in my life and what to do about it. Knowing what the Bible teaches didn't seem to rid me of my anger or change how it affects Joy.

Pastor: You are to be commended for working at understanding anger and how it affects your life and others. Knowledge does not always change behavior. It is often more complicated than that. I expect our sessions to help with that issue. It is my expectation that we will spend five sessions together over the next few weeks in which we will address issues related to anger. I'm committed to being as helpful as possible to you as the two of you seek to achieve understanding and to introduce whatever changes in your behavior you deem appropriate. If matters should come up that may be more effectively dealt with by someone else, we will discuss referral. Perhaps we could begin by your sharing how anger was expressed in your family of origin, and how you expressed your anger as you were growing up.

The pastor is here seeking to pick up and clarify the commitment made some weeks ago. In our discussion of "access points" in the first chapter, we indicated there were many possibilities. In his response to the announcement of the series on anger, Bill opened the discussion by focusing on the cognitive issue of understanding what the Bible says about anger. The pastor moved to a more personal discussion of anger and Bill acknowledged it as a personal problem. Now, some weeks later, as counseling begins it is important to clarify the access point at which they are prepared to begin. It is important to obtain commitment to the process, to affirm it, and to clarify any assumptions being made by the pastor. The attempt here is to place appropriate responsibility on Bill and Joy to work at what is important to them, and for them to assume responsibility for the changes they wish to see in their relationship.

At this point Bill proceeded to present his home as a place where anger was expressed freely, especially by his father and older brother. However, his mother held her own by yelling at the kids and banging the pots and pans. Everyone knew where she stood, but she got over it quickly and communicated warmth and acceptance in a good-humored way. Father, on the other hand, directed his energy into work and became a very successful person in the plant, obtaining the role of a foreman. This essentially led to Bill experiencing an absent father who modeled a strong commitment to work as the way to meet the needs of his family. Bill spoke of an older brother who seemed to be oppressive in Bill's experience, but this was not elaborated.

Pastor: That's helpful, Bill. We learn to express or not to express in our families of origin. It will be helpful for us to further understand how anger was experienced and expressed in your family. Many of the myths that we believe about anger and the masks we wear to cover anger are things learned in the context of our families. You will read about these in the book we will use in conjunction with these counseling sessions. It would be helpful if you could read the first couple of chapters of that book between now and our next session. That way, as we refer to these things, you will have that background and this will help us to maximize the effectiveness of this partnership we have entered into to look at your concerns about anger. Joy, were you aware of how anger was expressed in Bill's family?

Joy: Not really, but I can see he learned well. It sure was different in my family!

Pastor: (Ignoring the edge in her voice, but being aware of it, he chooses not to focus on it at this point.) The whole range of emotions is expressed differently in each family. The fruit of anger has a different look as it manifests itself in every family tree. Tell us how it was in your family with respect to anger.

Joy describes her home as a quiet, peaceful place where no one raised his or her voice and mother presided over things with good humor and efficiency, while father rather passively fulfilled his role as a very adequate provider. He was held in high esteem as a general medical practitioner and when at home retreated into quiet contemplation and music. Joy was the only child and was indulged considerably.

In this interchange the pastor has clarified further expectations, introduced the book that will guide them in understanding the content and process of counseling, and further reinforced the role they must assume in the counseling process. Also, in connection with what they have discussed about their families, he has introduced the concept of myths and masks, which may be elaborated as they learn about their experience and expression of anger.

Pastor: In short, it would appear there was not much anger evident and you had no one with whom to compete for attention. Life was pretty peaceful. You didn't have to cope with much anger and had little occasion to express it. Is that a fair description?

Joy: (In a wistful voice) I guess when one looks at it in summary, it was pretty peaceful.

Pastor: You sound a bit wistful, as if you wished that childhood state could be yours today. Maybe that provides a good transition to how it is today with you, Bill, Jeremy, and Shannon.

Joy: Oh, that's easy. Would you believe the difference is like day and night? I hate to complain, but I never have a moment's peace during the day. The kids are terribly demanding. And when Bill comes home he is always angry about something. I get frustrated. It just goes from bad to worse. I pray and it doesn't change anything. Sometimes I feel that God doesn't even hear, or doesn't care. Childhood was so peaceful and fun. There doesn't seem to be much of that anymore. I get pretty depressed at times.

Again, the pastor must be careful not to jump into issues that need to be explored but which are better left until later. The purpose at this point is to achieve an understanding of central concerns and to become aware of the wide range of relevant issues so that one can discern which would be most effectively addressed first. This is a time of understanding and exploration which provides the base for the strategy that will develop as the process unfolds. One may get the impression that Joy believes anger to be sin and to be caused by circumstances and other people, two of the myths discussed earlier. Also, the pastor has deliberately introduced the role of the children. One hypothesis that might come out of the previous comments would be that Joy expresses her anger more freely in relation to the children, wherein she is more overt, but appears to experience some guilt. On the other hand, she appears to withdraw or to be more subtle in expressing her anger toward Bill (her body language suggests anger and her withdrawal indicates a lack of freedom in expression) and has more need to project an image of "sweetness and light" in her relationship to adults as evidenced in her response to the pastor.

> *Pastor:* Well, the counseling session is a good place for us to hear about your frustration and anger. I suggest that not having had much anger expressed in your family may mean that you may not know how to express or respond to anger. We will need to explore that. However, your impression is that the contrast between what is and what used to be is dramatic. You carry a heavy load of responsibility at home. We will come back to talk about the relationship between your depression and the question of anger. Bill, what is the current situation for you at work and at home?
>
> *Bill:* Frankly, I'm in trouble in both places. At work the vice-president places unreasonable expectations on me. As supervisor of the plant, I have to meet quotas and production standards. The pressure is constant. I get angry and don't

know what to do with it. At home, if I express it I'm in trouble. Joy withdraws and I just get angrier. I don't know if a Christian is supposed to experience these things.

Pastor: If I can summarize and focus what the two of you are saying, it appears your concern is for your relationship with each other, with the children, and, in your case, Bill, with your work situation. In all of these relationships, anger appears to be the problem, either the experience of it, the expression of it (or lack of expression), and the way it impacts relationships. What we need to do, then, is to move toward clearly understanding what anger is, how we come to express it the way we do, and if there are better ways to do so. A second area of concern you mention has to do with where your Christianity fits into all of this. Let's look at this second question briefly. In our commitment to the Lord, we want to live in a way that demonstrates that commitment. We know we are "new creatures in Christ" but don't always feel that the "newness" seeps down into our behavior, at least not quickly enough. Sometimes it is not clear just what the Scripture teaches about some of these issues we struggle with day by day. Yet it is really important to each of us that somehow we incorporate and demonstrate our Christian faith in daily living. I really appreciate your desire to do this. Maybe we could start with a general question. How has your Christian commitment affected other areas of your life? Have you experienced some successes? And, how have you worked at making your faith relevant to your life, especially with reference to this matter of anger?

Conducting a Pastoral Diagnosis

This is another transition point in the session. When we use the term "diagnosis" we are doing so in a somewhat different way than the term would be used in a medical model. Perhaps the chief difference is that instead of focusing on the identification of pathology, we wish also to include the identification of strengths, gifts, or resources that will acknowledge the assets of the person and the grace of God operative in the life of the individual(s). Another way to express this is to focus on the spiritual well-being, as well as the difficulty the person may be having at this moment. We shift at this point to seek an understanding of the counselee's Christian commitment and how that is being worked out in relation to other areas of life, as well as to the issue at hand. Indeed, in some instances no relationship may be perceived or a great deal of tension may exist between one's life and one's faith commitment. It is important to provide opportunity to identify areas of success or achievement. Often it is helpful to ask one spouse to indicate the areas of strength that they see in the other person. This may help them to balance the problems or bruising experienced from the other with an acknowledgment that there are some things right in the relationship. An important measure for us is whether one spouse has the ability to acknowledge that which they can genuinely affirm in the other, or if they only choose to focus on the problems of the other. An obsession with problems, to the exclusion of the ability to acknowledge what is positive, is a strong contraindication of health. It is important to see the persons in terms of their whole experience rather than to see them strictly in terms of problems to be resolved. A pastor will want to affirm strengths, areas of giftedness, and areas of growth, as well as to deal with the problem areas.

> *Joy:* I felt really close to the Lord during the first few years after I became a Christian. I do get a lot of satisfaction from my work in the church teaching children. I feel less successful with my own children. I don't experience much anger. My problem is knowing how to respond to Bill's anger.
>
> *Pastor:* Many would affirm, Joy, that you are a gifted teacher and your contribution is appreciated. If we may, let's explore that a little. How did you maintain your closeness with the Lord during those years and how has that changed?
>
> *Joy:* Oh, we had devotions in our home, but I don't think I was really a Christian then, although I'm not even sure I knew that at that time. I was involved in Sunday school, and in high school I was in IVCF Bible study groups and the

church youth group. I went to summer camp. We had a great time. I loved all of that! At university, I was always with Christians. Now, I don't even have time for Bible reading, let alone prayer. I feel stuck in the house with little outside involvement, except Sunday.

Pastor: Much of your activity in spiritual things was in group activities with a great deal of fun and excitement. However, you had no clear commitment to the Lord at that time. Now, you feel stuck in a lonely situation with great responsibilities at home. Is that a fair summary?

Joy: Yes, in losing all of that I lost much of my excitement with Christianity even though much of that excitement was as a kind of spectator. Since becoming a Christian, I got off to a good start, but it has been downhill the last few years. At the moment, I don't cope well at home.

Pastor: You lost an experience of spiritual vitality and gained an experience of frustration and loneliness. Yet, you suggest you do not experience much anger and are only concerned about Bill's expression of anger. You talked earlier about some frustration in not knowing how to deal with the children when things get stressed. On the one hand, you are not sure that you are living up to your expectations of yourself as a Christian. On the other hand, you seem quite upset by Bill's behavior when he comes home and is not sensitive to where you are. I think I would call those responses anger. Are you at all aware of anger at those times?

The pastor's response at this point is an attempt to identify for Joy her response as a response of anger and to gently articulate the dissonance between her desire and commitment and the pattern that has come to characterize her response to the children and to Bill. Most of our readers will be aware of the early writings of Jay Adams (1970) and his discussion of Nouthetic Counseling. One might briefly define confrontation (*nouthesis*) as kindly but firmly bringing one another to the awareness of discrepancies or incongruity between our lives and the will of God to which we have committed ourselves. In this sense, confrontation may at times play a very large role in pastoral counseling. It is wise to assist a person in clarifying their commitment before they are helped to confront the dissonance in their lives with that commitment. At this early stage of the counseling relationship, one must be quite tentative.

Joy: But I don't yell or hit things. I'm frustrated but I want to be a good mom and a good wife. I feel that's my Christian responsibility. I saw that modeled in my home and I was raised in a Christian home.

Pastor: You do want to live out your Christian faith. You've evidenced that in your involvement in ministry in the church. Sometimes it is easier to be the Christian we want to be at church than it is at home. I would like to explore with you later your definition of anger and the frustration you experience in dealing with the kids and with Bill's anger. You mentioned earlier that you prayed about your situation. Has prayer and devotional reading been a part of your life?

Joy: (sadness in her voice) I try to be consistent. Sometimes I really feel in touch with God. Other times, like when we are having struggles, I'm not sure God is there. Since the kids have come along, I struggle more with finding time for private devotional time.

Pastor: It is a struggle to maintain one's expectations and hope for a devotional life. And, it does feel like God isn't there when we're uptight. Bill, are you able to find time in your pressured life to develop a devotional life and how does it affect the issues you struggle with?

Bill: Well, I don't do so well. It's only the last five years or so that I've been really trying to get into Christianity. I think a lot about God and talk to him some. But even though I think I've made some progress, I guess my spiritual life isn't what I'd like it to be, really.

Pastor: You feel that even though you have made some progress, your spiritual life has been blocked in some way? Can we explore that a little?

Bill: I don't know how much I understand that. I kind of expected that when I became a Christian my anger might go away. It is not clear to me how the changes I expect in my life as a Christian are to come about. I want to be a good Christian and a good husband. And I also need to be successful at work. Where does God fit into all of this? We hear about peace and joy in the Christian life, but we haven't experienced a lot of that. Is that our fault, or is this normal? Even knowing that the Bible says a lot about anger, I'm not sure how that all applies to my life. I sure hope we can get some answers. Well, there you are. I guess I spilled it out.

Pastor: You did spill it. You expressed intense feeling, perhaps we could call it anger, about not being able to make sense as to how the Christian faith should express itself in life. It sounds like this kind of expression is not usual for you, Bill. However, I bet it feels better than stuffing it down inside until it explodes in behavior you don't like.

Bill: Hey, you know, you're right. It does feel better.

In this situation, we have made the assumption that Bill and Joy are actively involved in the church and, therefore, assume that the pastor would have considerable knowledge of their family, their commitment to the fellowship of the church, and some sense of their spiritual journey.

In the above interaction, the pastor has learned much about Joy's perception of anger, but has chosen not to focus on that at this time. Joy has a rather limited repertoire as to the experience or expression of anger and appears to think of it in terms of "yelling or hitting." She does not see her frustration as anger, but focuses on Bill's anger and her not knowing how to respond. She apparently masks her anger with a pleasant exterior. She may mask anger by imploding and spiritualizing the experience.

She, at this point, does not see her participation in the problem with any clarity, but rather sees herself as a victim of circumstances. The circumstances are the children and her husband. She may accept the myth that anger is caused by circumstances and other people. She may also accept the myth that all anger is sin and that it is a spiritual issue having no place in a Christian home, since it was not evident in hers. She does see that her behavior is to express her Christian commitment and that she thought what was modeled in her family of origin represented

Christian living. The pastor focuses on her expressed desire to live out her Christian faith and her desire for more time for her spiritual life. It is not evident that her faith has either informed her relationship to Bill's anger or her relationship with her children, and she may be experiencing guilt as a result of not being able to experience the peace she saw in her parents. It would also appear that there is confusion between her understanding of spirituality and her experience of social excitement and fun as she experienced it in growing up associating with Christian youth. To define spirituality or Christianity in terms of the excitement and social involvement of youth may be very misleading.

Bill expresses a longing and a desire for God and for him to be relevant in his life. He apparently has not been able to bring his faith and his experiences of life into a satisfying relationship. However, he appears open. Bill began by believing the myth that the Bible has little to say about anger. In discovering that is not the case, he then struggles with the fact that knowledge is not sufficient in itself to effect the change he desires. Bill apparently accepts the myth that anger is primarily caused by circumstances or others. He saw evidence of the myth that anger is resolved by getting it off your chest in the behavior of his family. It would appear, also, that he has not effectively incorporated the disciplines of the Christian life into his daily experience.

It would be appropriate for the pastor to conclude this brief assessment of their spiritual journey and to transition to the next phase of this first session. In this transition, it will be helpful to affirm their spiritual pursuit by tentatively identifying issues that may be explored further in the following sessions. At the same time, one wishes to carefully move toward a consensus in which goals for the remaining sessions are mutually understood and accepted.

Pastor: I want to commend both of you for your evident interest in working at your relationship and the issues around anger and for your desire to apply your Christian faith to your lives and relationships. You have raised key questions about the relationship between anger and spirituality and how we incorporate and demonstrate our spiritual commitment in our lives. During the next few weeks, we will work together on this and, I believe, you will make good progress.

Achieving a Mutually Agreeable Focus for Counseling

As this session comes to a close, it is important to summarize and clarify directions for the coming sessions. It is important to articulate these in ways that capture the concern of Bill and Joy and, at the same time, to acknowledge that we will be moving to understanding that may challenge them and inform them that a plan of action will require their ownership and commitment.

Pastor: As we bring our session to a conclusion today, we need to summarize our concerns and clarify the direction we would like to take over the next few sessions. You have shared with me in a helpful way. I would like to give you some feedback from my perspective that may inform your subjective experience. It will be important for you to help me to define the way in which I can be most helpful to you as you chart new direction and change in your relationships. In attending the seminar sessions on anger, you acquired very helpful knowledge concerning what the Scripture teaches about anger, even if that knowledge did not bring immediate change. Obviously, both of you are concerned about your spiritual growth and development. Also, you want your relationship to each other, to your children, and your relationships at work, Bill, to be reflective of your Christian commitment. In all of these ways you have a strong foundation on which to build. Today we have begun to understand what you have learned about anger in your families and the differences that brings to each of your understandings and expression. This is important because anger is one of the fruits that grows on our family tree and it is different from family to family. In the light of new understanding and new experience, you will want to learn to express anger differently than you learned in your family. That is the task for these sessions, as I would understand it. Is that what you expect from these sessions?

Bill: When you put it that way, I experience a sense of relief.

Pastor: Maybe we could explore that a bit. Do you understand this sense of relief?

Bill: Well, I think it has to do with understanding that my anger behavior is learned and I came by it legitimately. It's not just that I'm bad in some way. It seems a bit more attainable to think of changing behavior. I'm not sure I know how to say it, but that makes a difference in the way I see Joy and I in our relationship. Maybe our behavior doesn't reflect our commitment very well. I don't think I understand that well, but it feels different.

Pastor: You have grasped a very important distinction, Bill. We need to explore and understand that more fully, but we've made a good start. Joy, how would you summarize any learning or new perspectives you've achieved?

Joy: Like Bill, I'm not very clear about what I think yet. But I have a sense that in spite of my family being such a wonderful place, maybe I didn't learn what it would be helpful to know about anger. Yet, I don't feel comfortable about being critical of my parents. Maybe my frustration with the kids and Bill is anger. I never thought of myself as angry, but only in terms of responding to Bill's anger or to the kids' behavior. I've got quite a bit of thinking to do about that. It's still fuzzy.

Pastor: Joy, entering into new learning is an experience of exploration. When you have explored new learning or entered into a new experience in the past you, like the rest of us, did so tentatively, cautiously, a kind of feeling of one's way. You will learn about your anger in the same way. The fact that things feel fuzzy and unclear now is OK. We should explore new thoughts and understandings with caution. Check it out and see if it fits. See if it feels like an accurate and helpful understanding. We need to explore further the feelings we experience around anger, but also look at the thought processes and the behavior that is expressed in anger. We need to look at the issue of anger and sin, pride, and the desire we experience for vengeance. We still have much to do, but we have made a good start. An important part of this process will be what you do between now and the next time we meet. I have some suggestions. This book that I will loan you (and which you can buy, if you wish) will provide much background material. I'd like you to read the first couple of chapters before next time. Also, I would like each of you to keep a rather simple journal. In that journal, I would like you to make short notes or outlines of situations during these next several days when you are conscious of experiencing anger. Note what you felt like, what you were thinking, and how you responded in terms of verbal or behavioral response. Also, I would like you both to read Mark 3:1–6 and reflect on it as it relates to you and our discussions. This is what we call homework, that thing we sometimes resisted in school. It will help immensely if you are faithful and conscientious in doing the homework. It will mean you will bring back to our sessions information that will be very valuable for our continued discussion. Your progress will be much greater and faster if you think through some of these things in between our sessions. Homework is very valuable in clarifying things and making the learning yours in a personal way. Does this seem reasonable to you?

Joy: I can anticipate having some difficulty in finding time, but I'd like to.

Bill: My schedule is going to be heavy too. But it would obviously be helpful.

Pastor: You are right. It will take time, but it will be valuable. Let me make a suggestion. Is there some way you could help each other to create the time necessary? For instance, could you alternate evenings when you are home, perhaps after the children are in bed? One evening Bill could keep a general ear open for the kids and help them to get settled in while Joy has an hour to do her homework. The next evening Joy could do that while Bill did his homework. It may require structuring things a little, but do you think you could organize in a way like that?

Bill: That sounds like a possibility to me.

Joy: I think so too.

Pastor: Good. Then, let's conclude today. We will plan to meet in a week and continue at that time.

4

SIN AND RIGHTEOUSNESS
SESSION 2

Summary: Session 2 begins with a connection to the first session and then moves to interaction around the various feelings that Bill and Joy are experiencing. From there the session moves to the biblical data on anger and into the question as to whether or not anger is sinful. This provides an important backdrop for the next session which will focus more on the thinking process.

Personal Preparation

Because the life of the pastor is busy and demanding, it is important to spend time in personal preparation before each counseling session. In the last session the pastor was late and rushed into the session. This can communicate inadvertently a lack of care or interest in the person and their problem. Even if there is not a large amount of time available, spend even a few minutes by yourself in your office to do four things:

1. Engage in quiet prayer and meditation. This will not only put you in the right frame of mind, but will also raise your awareness of the presence and involvement of God in the process.

2. Practice thought stopping. Many thoughts crowd into our minds during the day. These can serve as distractions during the counseling. Consciously set those thoughts to the side. Think of your mind as having a shelf where those thoughts can be left while you are talking to the person. This process will not guarantee a clear mind but it will move you in the right direction.

3. Review the details of the situation. What do you know about this situation? What happened in the last session? If you have taken notes, review those before the person comes in. Rehearse some of the salient details in your mind. This kind of preparation focuses you in on this specific situation and also communicates care in the session because you have the relevant information clear in your own mind. It is awkward to say something like, "What does your sister think of that?" only to find that this parishioner is an only child and it is your next person who has the controlling sister!

4. Put yourself in their situation. What would it be like to walk into a pastor's office, sit down, and talk about your personal life? What would it feel like to go to a pastor with your spouse to talk about personal struggles? What is it like to pass by the church secretary, the maintenance staff, and the day-care workers, then sit in the waiting room and anticipate a discussion about anger? These questions will vary from person to person and situation to situation, but the principle is consistent: seek to understand the parishioner's experience of coming for counseling.

Reconnecting with the Last Session

Pastor: It is good to see you again. I am wondering how both of you felt about our time together last week.

Joy: I am just exhausted today because I have been so busy and have had a cold the past three days, so it is hard to focus. I found our time to be helpful, even though it was a little hard to come and talk about such a personal subject. I struggled because I know Bill finds this kind of thing difficult. It is not easy for him to talk to someone about his problems.

Bill: Joy is right, but I know I need to be here. This anger topic has been eating away at me for too long. I should let you know that I really struggled with the homework, especially trying to think through the experience and the expression side of anger. I guess I have only focused on the expression side and never really thought too much about my experience. Your distinction between feeling, thinking, and behavior was quite new for me. But I was encouraged that Jesus got angry. I never knew I was just like Jesus!

The pastor has begun the session with an important question. It has been a week since he met with Bill and Joy. Given that there are 168 hours in a week, we can expect that the two of them will have had some reactions to the material that was discussed in the previous session. This discussion does not need to be lengthy but can perform a number of important functions in the counseling process.

1. Acknowledges that what goes on in between sessions is as important as what goes on in the counseling itself
2. Allows people to raise questions or concerns that are unresolved
3. Provides a soft measure as to whether the parishioner is motivated to deal with the concerns that have been raised
4. Gives the pastor the opportunity to check out some hunches or hypotheses that may have formed since the last session
5. Allows for repetition or rehearsal of some of the salient issues from the last time
6. If the person left the office with an unclear thought or feeling, it allows the pastor to address it right at the beginning of the next session

7. Provides continuity and emphasizes that the counseling is a process over time rather than disconnected isolated events

It is necessary for the pastor to determine what is important and should be addressed and what is not important and should not be addressed. This requires discernment and a willingness to make decisions. For instance, he may want to acknowledge her exhaustion and cold, but this is not the place to get off on tangents. Strategic Pastoral Counseling is time limited, so their concerns around anger need to be the prime focus. Notice that this is in contrast to a social setting, where friends might want to explore where she got the cold and why she is so busy. It is also in contrast to more long-term psychotherapy, where there may be some examination of busyness as a defense or a perception that social talk may reflect resistance.

Discussing the Homework

Since one of the outcomes of homework is the reinforcement of material discussed in the previous session, the reference to the homework should be not a surprise.

Pastor: Maybe both of you can walk me through the first part of the assignment. Let's start with you, Joy. Can you describe the situations where you were angry and tell me about your experience and expression of that?

Joy: I had four situations in total. One of them involved a problem between Bill and me, but the other three involved Jeremy and Shannon. I know they are only seven and two but they seem to be at odds all the time. In all three situations I felt like I was mildly irritated. I try to stay cool and calm but sometimes it is hard to simply grin and bear it. I feel totally drained and can hardly move on to the next task.

Pastor: So, for you the experience of anger builds and is felt very deeply, but you are not sure how to express it?

In the early stages of the counseling process, it is important for the pastor to avoid a very natural tendency to jump in and solve all the problems or answer all the questions. Joy has described some situations that will require intervention. For instance, a grin-and-bear-it approach to anger is often not very productive, but now is not the time to pursue this avenue. In contrast, the pastor has made a brief summary statement which communicates empathy. The pastor is present in the situation, listening carefully and offering an empathic response. What is empathy? Empathy is the ability to understand what someone is experiencing (i.e. thoughts, feelings, ideas, and so on) and communicate that understanding back to them. In doing this, you not only communicate care but you may help them understand what they are experiencing in more depth and detail.

Joy's comments could have produced a number of minisermons on ways to resolve sibling rivalry, the developmental differences between two year olds and seven year olds, or the pros and cons of staying cool in anger. What the pastor did was focus on the big picture that came out of the homework, namely, what was your experience and expression of anger in various situations during the week? Even though Joy had not used the terms "experience" or "expression," his summary statement wove them in. And most importantly, he did not just think about what she said and seek his own internal understanding, he verbalized what he heard. This is the key to empathy. Empathy is not just a reception skill focused on what I have heard. It is also a communication skill, in that I seek to communicate what I have heard back to the person. This allows them to clarify, refine, or negate my understanding, and potentially allows them to have fuller insight about what they have said.

In short-term counseling, there is no time to deal with all the homework in the session. This is not a problem since the utilization of homework communicates that the parishioner has some responsibility in the process as well, and what goes on outside the session has value. The pastor has simply asked Joy to tell him about the situations where she was angry and how she experienced and expressed this anger. Some people will bring in pages of notes in response to this request, while others may have a superficial analysis of one situation. What is important is the thematic analysis of the homework. The pastor's empathic summary achieved that goal. If he is wrong in what he said, Joy will probably bring in some new information from the week. If he is right, she will be able to look at the rest of the homework through the experience-expression grid.

Focusing on Feelings

> *Pastor:* Bill, you have already expressed that you found the homework difficult. Tell me about your journaling of situations where you were angry.
>
> *Bill:* It's funny. I could only think of one situation during the week. Actually, it is the same one that Joy referred to. But I have felt angry most of the time. Is that possible? Can you be feeling angry without it being tied to a particular event?
>
> *Pastor:* Those are important questions, but let's put them on hold for a moment. Help me understand your feelings of anger. What were you experiencing in the one situation? Was that different from what you were experiencing the whole week?

The pastor has provided a good balance in his response. On the one hand, he has acknowledged Bill's questions and affirmed their importance. On the other hand, the focus of the discussion is on Bill's experience with anger during the week. To begin discussing some of the theoretical issues tied to anger is to miss Bill at a personal level. People sometimes avoid dealing with feelings by flipping into more cognitive, abstract approaches. This is a particularly easy trap for pastors to fall into as they can start to advise/direct and provide biblical solutions (i.e. he should not be angry all week!). Bill's questions are important, but they need to be postponed until the feelings are understood both by the pastor and by Bill.

Bill: The only situation that I noted was from last Thursday when I came home from the plant. I had told Joy before going to work that I had a really important meeting and when I came home I expected her to ask me how it went. I came in the door, asked her how she was, and she went into this long and rambling description of her day. I was pretty incensed because I thought she had more care and interest in me. I expected to be cared for and she seemed more preoccupied with herself.

Joy: Well, I had experienced a tough day as well. I was going to ask about your meeting, but you came in and asked me how my day was. I assumed you were interested and wanted to know!

Bill: I did want to know, but I did not think it would take ten minutes!

Joy: It wasn't ten minutes. You always exaggerate when you're angry!

Bill: (is quiet and grunts silently)

These situations often create great discomfort for pastoral counselors. The feelings are intense and there does not seem to be any resolution to them. Anger is sitting out in the open with tremendous ambiguity attached to it. It may remind pastors of what goes on in board meetings at times. A heated topic comes up for discussion and conflict is brought to the surface. Some in the meeting are not deterred by the expression of feeling, while others try to avoid it or cover it up. At times the phrase "let's keep feelings out of this" is used as a weapon to keep the feelings at bay. Somehow everyone is supposed to be logical and rational, and approach these emotionally laden events without any feelings. Typically, this is a recipe for a restless night and a flat following day.

It is important for the pastor to have enough self-understanding and insight to be able to process his/her own reactions to the strong expression of feeling in Bill and Joy. This requires that pastors learn to trust their own experience and tune in to what is going on inside. Oscar Wilde said it well: "To reject one's own experience is to arrest one's own development and to deny one's own experience is to put a lie into the lips of one's own life and it is no less than the denial of the soul." This process of understanding your own reactions can be done in three different ways.

1. Head chatter: what is going on in your head at this moment (i.e. thinking, judging, planning, remembering, anticipating, analyzing, and so on)?
2. Body awareness: what are you experiencing in your body (i.e. fear, anxiety, discomfort, peace, tranquillity, rest, and so on)?
3. Historical links: does this remind you of anything in your own history (i.e. what happened when people got angry in your home? what were the family rules on anger?)?

A helpful response would be characterized by an absence of challenge and a willingness to stay with what the couple is feeling. This is important and valuable information. You are not talking about anger theoretically anymore but are seeing it live and in color. This is very helpful to the counseling process. There is no need to worry about the explanation at this stage or be concerned with solutions or side taking. The clear expression of feeling is very helpful to the whole process. Even when the pastor is uncomfortable with this direct expression of feeling, there should be a concerted effort to tune in to what others are experiencing and respond empathically.

Pastor: We talked in our last session about the importance of understanding our experience and expression of anger. My impression is that both of you are experiencing anger over this situation. Bill, you said you were pretty incensed at the time and I get the feeling that you are experiencing it again at this point.

Bill: You're right. When the problem escalated on Thursday and I told Joy why I was upset, she started getting defensive and telling me about her busy day. That just made me more upset. And now she is back into that approach again. I can feel the anger welling up inside me.

Pastor: Bill, you seemed to back off or shut down when you and Joy got into the conflict a few minutes ago. She said you always exaggerate when you are angry. You appeared to slump into the chair, gave a little grunt, and went quiet. And, yet, I assume you were still angry. Do you sometimes express your anger in passivity and withdrawal?

Making observations of what is happening in the office involves some risk, but can be stated with more tentative phrases. For the pastor to say that Bill seemed to back off is not to draw a definitive conclusion, but to make a suggestion that can be confirmed or denied. This intervention also helps to bring the problem into the present experience, rather than something the couple is talking about. Sometimes in counseling you find yourself listening to people describing and relaying their experience and you have no way of knowing what really happened. When Bill and Joy live out a conflict in front of the pastor, there is an opportunity to move from the descriptive to the real.

In the first session, the pastor talked about anger from the standpoint of thinking, feeling, and behavior. Often feelings are the best way into understanding the problem because that is the level that people live at experientially. Later on in the counseling, there will be a greater focus on Bill and Joy's thoughts and values, as well as their behaviors. Note, however, that the pastor is trying to stay with the feelings and is not moving into a judgment or analysis of them. This will not only increase the pastor's understanding of the problem, but will give the couple a sense that they are being cared for and understood. If the pastor was to ignore the feelings and rush to solutions, it would appear to be canned and generic and not really tuned in to Bill and Joy's experience of the anger.

> *Bill:* Do you remember when I talked to you at the back of the church and I said that I was not sure how to express my anger? That is exactly what happens to me. I am afraid to let it out in case I lose control. On the other hand, stuffing it inside is frustrating as well. What you just saw is one of my strategies. I go quiet and withdraw.
>
> *Joy:* I find it difficult when you do that because I know you are still angry, but you won't level with me and tell me what

is going on. I start feeling rejected and that makes my anger get deeper. I suppose I also have a battle when you just let it all out and you do not seem to know why you are so upset. But then I struggle to get it out myself and let you know what is going on.

Pastor: It is interesting that you display a pattern that we often see in men and women. When they are angry, men seem to find it easier to withdraw to avoid the conflict. In contrast, women tend to seek out the relationship and want to deal with it directly.

There is a lot of information on the table, a fair number of feelings are being expressed, and the couple is starting to reveal some of their thoughts and values. It is important for the pastor to acknowledge that at times counseling is overwhelming and accept that as a given. It is also important to resist the temptation to remove the ambiguity and complexity. At this stage, the pastor could find it easy to give them a line that would be an attempt to pacify them, not with their interest in mind but with the resolution of his own discomfort as the goal. Sometimes when people are overwhelmed with what they are being told, they offer a well-intentioned, simple line: "Well, things could be a lot worse," "Maybe you should pursue professional help," "If you just . . ." or "I will pray for you." The pastor needs to summarize what he/she is hearing and move them on. Being directive is important in this style of counseling.

Understanding the Biblical Data

Pastor: There is a lot on the table right now. I am hearing each of you struggling with anger, both individually and in your relationship. It seems like understanding what you are feeling and expressing that directly to your partner is not very easy at times. It also seems that you have different styles in dealing with the anger. Joy, you seem to keep it to yourself a lot of the time, but just a few minutes ago you got irritated with Bill. Bill, you find it easy to dump your anger out, especially in light of your family background, but pulling back into yourself is a way to avoid this. These different styles make it difficult for you to understand each other. What I would like to do is move to the other part of your homework. We will get back to some of the issues you raised, but I want to focus our attention on the passage in Mark 3. Joy, tell me about your reflections on the passage.

Joy: When I read the passage it reminded me of my church experience growing up. Many of the people were very legalistic and picky about minor issues. It was interesting to see how Jesus responded to them.

Pastor: In what sense was it interesting?

Joy: Well, his anger and frustration at them for missing the big picture.

Pastor: I don't know if you have ever thought this through or not, but it is easy to read the Bible simply as words on a page and forget that these are historical events that actually happened. As we read it, I would like you to plug in your biblical VCR unit for a moment and describe for me what the scene looks like when Jesus gets angry.

As Christian counselors, we recognize that the Scriptures are both a light and a lamp (Ps. 119:105) to bring us into truth. The teaching we receive is given "so that through endurance and the encouragement of the Scriptures we might have hope" (Rom. 15:4). By affirming these values, we acknowledge that the Scriptures are "living and active" (Heb. 4:12). In asking Bill and Joy to think about the biblical image, the pastor is not only directing them to the text, but is affirming that the story is alive and vital, not static and stale. The interaction with Jesus and the religious leaders took place in a historical context. There is a human, earthy quality to the narrative that taps into their own experience. While there are cognitive lessons to be learned from the story, the humanness is important at this stage in the interaction. Anger has a relational and sensual quality to it. What better place to look for understanding than the pages of the Bible?

Joy: When I think of what I can see in this story, I see Jesus in a long white robe in front of this large synagogue. There is a mob of people hanging around and off to the side is a man with a shriveled hand sitting in a heap beside a wall. At that moment there is a pause in the action as Jesus looks at the man and some of the people around them start looking at Jesus. Jesus invites the man to stand up and everyone seems stunned like something significant is going to happen. Jesus speaks to them sternly and asks them about their view of the Sabbath and whether it is right to do good on the Sabbath. Then he looks at them with sadness and weariness and tells the man to stretch out his hand.

Bill: That's very different than what I see in the story. Jesus is really ticked and angry and he lets them have it. He cannot stand the hypocrisy in these religious people. They make his blood boil!

The different responses of Joy and Bill illustrate the various ways that people will process Scripture. Joy has gone into elaborate detail as to how the incident unfolded. In contrast, Bill has missed the nuances of the story and focused in on the anger of Jesus. Both of them have read their own experiences and history into the biblical story. While pastors often understand this dynamic in preaching, they may not be as comfortable when it comes out in the office. It may appear that people are not bowing to the authoritative nature of Scripture or are making God's Word secondary to their own experience. However, when people are asked to reveal their implicit view of biblical stories we are able to understand where they are much more definitively.

At the beginning of the session, Bill voiced his encouragement that Jesus got angry too. What he has done is to take his own experience of anger and find validation for it in Scripture. In essence, the experiential becomes foundational and the Scriptures provide support. While this approach does not meet theological criteria regarding an accurate view of Scripture, it gives the pastor a clear sense of how Bill and Joy are processing the biblical material. Having discovered that, he can then move toward Scripture being foundational and having an influence on their experience and expression.

Pastor: It is interesting to see the different ways that you have seen this story. Joy, you see Jesus as being weary and sad while, Bill, you see Jesus as having much more intense and passionate feelings. Why do you think you view this situation so differently?

Joy: In many ways we have just described our own anger. I am much more passive and quiet about my anger. I tend to get weary and sad when I am upset with someone. Bill, on the other hand, tends to let it fly more. In fact, this issue has come up before when we did a Bible study on Jonah. One particular night we decided to act out the story and Bill was given the role of playing Jonah in the fourth chapter. You know, the one where Jonah is upset with God and then God teaches him a lesson through a vine? Well, Bill went berserk in this role. It fit him to a T! In fact, people were totally taken aback by his expression of anger.

Bill: The interesting thing was that many people did not see the passage in the same way. They saw Jonah as mildly irritated and thought he expressed his frustration quietly in a somber prayer.

Pastor: What you are describing is a variation in the feelings that different people experience when they feel angry. Let's explore this a little further. If I can be simple for a moment, most of our feelings are experienced from the neck down. It is our body that allows us to experience emotions. For example, when I am anxious I feel myself get tight in my chest and my throat feels dry. In fact, this is one way that I find out I am anxious. Sometimes my body communicates it before my mind forms the thought "I am anxious."

It is the same with anger. I will feel a very tight knot in the pit of my stomach and I will notice that my breathing is somewhat forced and intermittent. I have been in meetings where these physical reactions have been occurring and when I tune in to that and realize they are present, I then realize that I am angry.

The pastor has done a number of things well in this intervention. First, he has linked feelings with physical reactions. Feelings are not thoughts or attitudes, but are emotional responses that are resident in the body. The body then can become a cue to what is happening. But note the way the pastor communicated this issue. He used self-disclosure and co-pilgrimage as a way of communicating truth. It would have been easy to lapse into a theoretical treatise, but instead he has linked himself with Bill and Joy by describing his own bodily reactions for both feelings in general and anger more specifically. In communicating his humanness, the pastor is aligning himself with those who he is helping and providing validation of what they are talking about. Further, the research on self-disclosure indicates three major outcomes of utilizing this approach in counseling (Watkins, 1990): (1) higher counselor ratings by the counselee, (2) greater self-disclosure by the counselee, and (3) greater willingness by the counselee to continue with the counseling.

It is important to remember that self-disclosure always has the good of the other in mind. Pastoral counseling does not provide an opportunity for the pastor to spill all his/her issues and concerns. The focus is on the growth and development of the parishioner. If personal sharing is going to accomplish that goal, then it is appropriate.

Joy: I find it odd that you are talking so much about feelings. I guess, if I am honest, I thought that Christians were not supposed to go with their feelings. In fact, I read a tract once that said we should start with faith, then move to facts, and let the feelings follow after. That seems to make feelings unimportant, almost insignificant. Then I was listening to this Christian radio program the other day and the speaker said that we cannot trust our feelings. I am not sure how to put all this together.

Bill: I'm with Joy. Every time I feel strongly about something, this little voice says that I am wrong and need to repent. But then I look at the example of Jesus and of Jonah and think that feelings cannot be all bad.

Pastor: You have raised some very important questions about feelings. Let's explore this a little further. Unfortunately, there are a lot of confusing messages about feelings in Christian circles and this has created difficulty for many people. I like to use three terms to help people understand this area: acknowledge, accept, and approve. First of all, it is very important to acknowledge that we have feelings. If we are not honest with ourselves, before God, we are missing what is actually happening. To acknowledge feeling is really to describe reality—this is the way things are right now. The next step is to accept what we are feeling. Often people will acknowledge in a grudging way that they are experiencing emotion, but will have trouble accepting particular feelings. I remember talking to a woman who had lost her husband to cancer. She could acknowledge that she was feeling something, but could not accept the fact that she was angry. Somehow anger was not right. It was sinful and unacceptable.

Bill: That is exactly what goes on inside me. I know that I am feeling deeply, but then when I realize it is anger I struggle admitting to it because I think it is wrong. I spend so much time trying to fight it off that it stresses me out. Eventually I cannot take it anymore and my anger comes out in extreme ways. How can I avoid this?

Pastor: Bill, you are getting acceptance and approval mixed up. Accepting that you are angry is not a statement about whether you approve of it or not. For example, I accept the fact that I sin, but I do not approve of it. Before I came to faith in Christ, I had to accept the fact that I was an enemy of God. That was a necessary first step before I could repent of my sin and come to Christ. To accept that you are angry is only to say, "This is the way things are right now." This kind of acceptance requires an integrity and an authenticity that describes reality for what it is. Having done that, you are ready to reflect on the area of sin and righteousness, or, in the language that we have been using, you are ready to decide if you approve or disapprove of the way things are.

Joy: As I listen to you, I think I am getting a clearer picture about my response to anger. I think my problem starts at the acknowledgment stage. I have trouble acknowledging that I have feelings. I am often more concerned about thoughts, ideas, and concepts. When anger does come, I try to downplay it and deny it. I put on a happy face and grin and bear it. In a sense, I do not allow myself to experience anger because I do not want to feel.

Pastor: Again, I sense some differences between you in how you understand anger. Bill, you are worried that your anger will be sinful so you have trouble accepting it. In contrast, Joy, you are not quite sure how to acknowledge your feelings in general so anger is something that is hard to integrate into your view of yourself.

Bill: But how does all this tie to sin?

The pastor has validated their concerns by indicating that they are not alone. He is not defensive about the Christian community, but is willing to acknowledge that there are confusing messages about feelings. This is important, particularly for relatively new Christians who may not know how to understand the implicit messages in evangelical culture. However, the pastor has not turned this into a critique but has moved to three simple words to help Bill and Joy understand feelings in general. Taking a threefold concept like acknowledge, accept, and approve can give people handles on dealing with complex problems. The key is that these terms are simple, but not simplistic, and they are sufficiently basic that Bill and Joy will be able to utilize them in the future.

This interaction was teaching oriented, but involved partnership and participation. Often these terms—teaching, partnership, and participation—do not go together. Normally, pastors communicate truth from a distance in the pulpit and the opportunity for interaction and participation are nonexistent. While this may be an acceptable style for a traditional sermon, the danger is that some pastors will adopt this style in counseling. Strategic Pastoral Counseling is directive, but this does not mean that the pastor should move into a sermonic style. Often, like in this situation, the parishioner's contribution is a key component in getting a concept explained.

While Jesus both taught and embodied truth, he often communicated in an interactive style. Even in his first recorded teaching time he is "sitting among the teachers, listening to them and asking them questions" (Luke 2:46). His teaching on condemning others' sin took place when his formal teaching time was interrupted by the Pharisees bringing in a woman caught in adultery (John 8:1–11). It is easy for pastors to lose sight of the fact that sermons are only one way of communicating truth. Truth in the biblical sense is not obscure and abstract. It is not distant and removed. It is personal and relational. The pastor has demonstrated this reality in the counseling session. It is because of this view of truth that Jesus could summarize the Law in two commandments which are inherently relational:

> Love the Lord your God with all your heart and with all your soul and with all your mind and with all your strength. . . . Love your neighbor as yourself. (Mark 12:30–31)

Anger: Right or Wrong?

Pastor: When we get into the realm of sin and righteousness we are really asking two questions. Does God approve of the anger? Do I approve of the anger? Part of our struggle as Christians is to achieve harmony between the answers to these two questions. If God sees our anger as sinful, then we need to repent of it and strive against it. On the other hand, if God does not disapprove of our anger, then we should not beat ourselves up over it. Let's go back to Mark 3. Does Jesus' anger seem like sin to you?

Bill: I know that it is not sin because it is Jesus experiencing it, but I see him as really ticked, angry, and his blood is boiling. When I am like that it seems sinful.

Joy: I don't see a strong display of emotion in this passage, more the weariness and sadness I talked about earlier. I have never really thought about whether it is sin or not.

This conclusion is a reality for many people. Some, who have trouble acknowledging feelings, do not even think about the sin and righteousness question. They are so concerned to deny what they are feeling out of their family history that the morality side of it is relatively unimportant. Given Joy's background of seeing little expression of feeling, it is not surprising that she does not see it here. On the other hand, people like Bill who constantly link anger and sin are unable to see past the sin and consider that anger could be righteous. Even their reading of Jesus in this passage is to "read it" as sinful. In Strategic Pastoral Counseling, the pastor acknowledges and seeks to understand the feelings that are being expressed, but the emotional side does not become the moral touchstone. Rather, morality needs to be understood with reference to biblical data.

Pastor: Let me try to summarize some of the key biblical issues when it comes to sin and righteousness. First, it is important to realize that the Bible does not say that all anger is right or wrong. It really depends on the passage that we are looking at and the situation that is under consideration. You referred to the example of Jonah and his anger at God. It is interesting that God asked him if he had any right to be angry. In that situation it appears that God was unhappy with Jonah's emotional expression. Jonah was frustrated because God had been compassionate and had not brought the destruction on Nineveh that he had promised. In contrast, you have Paul's words in 2 Corinthians 7. He is encouraging the Corinthians to engage in godly sorrow, a quality that is characterized by indignation, alarm, concern, and a readiness to see justice done. Interestingly, the word he uses for indignation is a word that is in the "angry" family and means irritation. Here Paul is praising this kind of emotive response. Then, as parents, you may remember what Paul said in Ephesians 6 in talking about parental responsibilities toward children. He warns that parents should not exasperate or discourage their children. Here the children are feeling that deep sense of frustration because their parents are not responding in an appropriate manner. Finally, you are no doubt aware of many of the passages on God's wrath. Do you remember when Jesus talked about those who reject him in John 3? He talked about them as those who had God's wrath resting on them.

Bill: That's interesting. I didn't realize that anger was so complex in the Bible.

Joy: This may sound strange, but I have never connected God's wrath with anger. You know how sometimes you repeat a word over and over but never really stop to think what it means? That has happened for me with God's wrath. I have not made a conscious connection between his wrath and human anger.

The pastor's biblical teaching on anger is excellent as he has avoided the danger of dumping all of it on Bill and Joy. Such an approach would be overwhelming and would lead to confusion, not clarification. He has taken a few key points and a few themes. The goal is to show the diversity in the biblical material and to set the stage for them to do more work on their own. What is being said here is only a summary. Bill and Joy have a grid that they can bring to the material that will be encountered later on in the process.

Ideally, it is helpful if the pastor has this material committed to memory so that it can be recalled spontaneously. This strategy makes the counseling process more natural and interactive and allows the pastor to quote the biblical material in a way that captures the sense rather than giving it word for word in detail. The utilization of an open Bible is not wrong in the counseling process, but at this stage the merging of biblical material into the relational climate of the interaction is ideal.

These concerns raise questions about the importance of Scripture in the counseling process. There are four ways in which we can understand the role of Scripture in this environment.

1. Live the Scriptures out in our lives so we become representatives of it in character and communal style. The words of 1 Peter 3:1: "if any of them do not believe the word, they may be won over without talk by the behavior of their

wives" indicate that righteous living that is in step with God's truth is communicated in behavior, not just in cognitive assertion. This viewpoint gives Paul the confidence to say in Philippians 4:9: "Whatever you have learned or received or heard from me, or seen in me—put it into practice."

2. Have a clear sense of the overall tenor of Scripture. Being conversant with overall biblical themes like salvation, redemption, sin, suffering, justification, comfort, and the like will allow pastors to bring a big picture perspective to the particular concerns that people bring to counseling. This moves the biblical perspective into a broader umbrella of God's message over time and history, rather than a detailed analysis of particular passages. This approach would utilize the Book of Deuteronomy as a powerful illustration of the significance of history and the fact that behavior and consequences cannot be separated. Or the wisdom literature might be employed as an illustration that the fear of the Lord works itself out in human relationships and that an understanding of God demands healthy functioning.

3. Work at developing a clear understanding of the specific problem areas addressed in Scripture with a recognition that some of these areas have led to differences in interpretation. When parishioners come for counseling, they will probably assume that one of the strengths that the pastor will bring to the interaction will be clarity on the Bible's position on a given issue. If the pastor is going to counsel Bill and Joy with professional competence, he will need to be sure that he has a good understanding of the biblical perspective on anger. Believing in the power of Scripture: "All Scripture is God-breathed and is useful for teaching, rebuking, correcting and training in righteousness" and the result of that power: "so that the man of God may be thoroughly equipped for every good work" (2 Tim. 3:16–17) demands that the pastor be "a workman who does not need to be ashamed and who correctly handles the word of truth" (2 Tim. 2:15).

4. Recognize that not all contemporary difficulties are addressed specifically in the Bible, but the principles of Scripture can bring understanding and resolution. For example,

a sixteen-year-old girl who is struggling with bulimia and anorexia cannot be pointed to a specific verse that directly speaks to her difficulty. The middle-aged Christian man who is fighting a battle with a fragile identity after losing his job will not be able to locate a particular passage that is exhaustive in its understanding of his problem. However, biblical principles that focus on the body (1 Cor. 6:12–20) may begin to address the teen's problem and the man may find some important understanding in the fact that his life "is now hidden with Christ in God" (Col. 3:3).

Joy: You really need the Holy Spirit in your life to determine when anger is right and when it is wrong.

Pastor: I am with you on that point, Joy, but I wonder if you have ever thought about how the Holy Spirit becomes our teacher and counselor.

Bill: Doesn't the Holy Spirit intercede for us when we are praying? Is that how he becomes our teacher and counselor?

These are the moments in counseling when the pastor can embarrass people and make them feel like they do not know much. Second Timothy 2:25 refers to the Lord's servants as those who must "gently instruct." That is what is needed here. Joy knows the Holy Spirit plays a role and Bill has some vague understanding of the teaching about the Holy Spirit in Romans 8. This area has been opened up by Joy, and the pastor followed it up with a good question.

Pastor: In John's Gospel, chapter 15 and verse 26, Jesus says that the Holy Spirit is the counselor who will teach all things and remind us of everything that Jesus said. I believe the Holy Spirit can bring the truths of Scripture to life. He can also guide us so that we do not fulfill the lusts of the flesh, but walk in his truth. He reveals God to us and what God has given us. He also gives gifts to believers so that they can minister and reach out to others with God's truth. Frankly, I find all of this very reassuring and helpful when it comes to pastoral counseling. I have a very deep sense that

I am not doing this alone, but because I am filled with the Holy Spirit I bring a powerful dynamic to our time together. I also take great comfort in the fact that your struggles with anger can be addressed by Scripture as revealed by the Holy Spirit.

Sometimes people will pit the Holy Spirit against counseling. Since the Holy Spirit is my teacher and counselor, I can go on my own with him. However, the Holy Spirit works with Scripture and with others to bring people to a knowledge of truth. The Holy Spirit's demonstration at Pentecost was in the context of the community of believers meeting together. The work of the Holy Spirit is an empowering in the body. Pastoral counselors, doing their work under God and in step with the Holy Spirit, are those that are following his moving. This truth is often misunderstood because people assume that the opposite of self-help—I can do everything on my own and in my own strength—is that God does everything—no one has to do anything because God does everything. A full understanding of the empowerment that comes through the Holy Spirit produces the realization that all the good any of us do comes from his work in our lives. The active work of the Holy Spirit in counseling is enabling and energizing for both the pastor and the parishioner.

Pastor: Let's go back to the link between anger and sin. I would like to talk a little bit about a passage found in Ephesians 4. You may have heard this section quoted before, but I would like to explain it in some detail. Paul says in verses 26 and 27: "'In your anger do not sin': Do not let the sun go down while you are still angry, and do not give the devil a foothold." Let's look at this a phrase at a time. What does "in your anger do not sin" mean to each of you?

Bill: I guess it implies that you can be angry and deal with it in a sinful way or a nonsinful way. Maybe you can be angry for the right reason but express it in the wrong way.

Joy: I have never understood that phrase. Is it talking about our experience of anger or our expression?

Pastor: You have both raised some important issues. Bill, you are right in your understanding of the passage. It does indicate that you can be angry in a sinful way or a nonsinful way. Joy, your question is an important one and it takes us to the next phrase: "Do not let the sun go down while you are still angry." Paul is indicating that you can nurture and cultivate your anger in such a way that it persists over time. That is really the sense of the sun going down. We need to deal with our anger and not let it fester. If we do that, we are giving the devil a foothold. In other words, poorly managed anger provides an opportunity for the devil.

Bill: That certainly is my experience. When I read Ephesians 6 about the spiritual battle, I often think of my struggle with anger. I am not making this overly mysterious, but I really feel a deep bondage that seems to go beyond straight feelings. It is almost as if I am in a fierce battle that I have no control over. My mind is plagued by angry thoughts and I think about lashing out at people.

Pastor: I don't want to lose what you have just said, Bill, but our time is up for tonight. Because anger has a feeling, thinking, and behavioral component, it is not surprising that you have moved naturally into talking about your thoughts. Let me suggest that we revisit what you have mentioned about your thought life in our next session together. Tonight we have focused more on feelings and experience along with a beginning on the issue of sin and righteousness. I would like to give you some homework that builds on what we have discussed tonight and also prepares you for next time.

Homework

Pastor: I would like both of you to do some journaling prior to the next session. This will focus on the thought processes that accompany experiences of anger. When you experience anger, ask questions like: How am I talking to myself? What do I tell myself? What kinds of images come to mind when

I reflect on my thoughts toward myself? Do I feel trapped? boxed in? sick to my stomach? want to kick myself around the block? This assignment is an attempt to capture, even in a sketchy way, the appraising of one's self in the experience of anger. The other side of the thought process is what I think of my spouse. Is there imagery that would capture these thoughts? Do I wish he/she would stay away? Do I hope he/she has an accident? What animal would best picture the other person, as I experience their response? What meaning do I attribute to their actions, words, and expressions? I would also like you to read Numbers 13:26–33 and focus on the attitudes of the spies toward themselves. Then look at Jonah 4:1–10 and reflect on the difference between Jonah's perspective and God's. I would like you to do your biblical study independently. Sometimes in a marital situation it is helpful to have the spouses do this kind of Bible study on their own and then have them share their thoughts with each other. When you share with each other, focus on acceptance and a pursuit of the other person's understanding and perspective on the passage. This is not a time to convince or persuade to a different perspective.

5

PRIDE AND HUMILITY
SESSION 3

Summary: Session 3 moves into a more in-depth discussion on the relationship between feeling and thinking. Family of origin issues are introduced as an important component of understanding the process of anger. Pride is presented as an absolutizing of our experience so that our perspective is the only one. The anger of some biblical characters, as well as that of God, is utilized to illustrate the points. These issues provide a good backdrop for the behavioral emphasis of session 4.

Clarifying a Plan for the Session

Again, let us reiterate the importance of having a preparatory time for the session. It will be very important to organize one's thoughts and intention in preparation for the session. One must reconnect with the previous session through reflecting on the hypotheses generated as a result of the previous two sessions. It is not helpful to fly freely from session to session without clear connection. The depth of your care and the seriousness with which you take their issues will be clearly evidenced by their understanding that you have thoughtfully and prayerfully considered their situation between sessions.

The plan for this session is outlined here as an example. Obviously, one must be open and responsive to any startlingly new developments brought to the session. However, we are not practicing nondirective counseling, but, rather, a structured approach which has more ready application to the role of a counseling pastor. One of the strengths of the structured approach is its contractual nature coupled with a mutually agreed upon focus. The commitment that characterizes it is mutual and brings direction and more clarity of expectation than does psychoanalytical or more nondirective approaches. This permits a general preplanning of sessions which, of course, must be coupled with a sensitive response to the counselee(s). The commitment to the focus or agenda for counseling provides the rationale for avoiding the tangents that so frequently pop up and have the potential of distraction. The discipline of staying with the counseling focus agreed upon may be quite freeing and makes the time-limited process a realistic approach. Since we are projecting five sessions, we need to have clarity of direction and gently, but firmly, keep to the commitment that was made in session 1.

Session 1 accomplished some bonding between the pastor and parishioner, differentiating counseling from other pastoral functions, exploring some relevant history, making some minimal pastoral diagnoses to supplement the pastor's fairly extensive knowledge of the couple, and establishing a focus for counseling with some explicit parameters. Session 2 moved into the engagement stage, introducing and focusing on the affective dimensions in the experience of anger, helping Bill and Joy to acknowledge and accept feelings and to understand the difference between acceptance and approval. They were helped to become aware of their different responses and to see that biblical data explicates their experience. The issue of anger as sin or the expression of righteousness was dealt with.

In Session 3, it would be appropriate to move to the exploration of anger in its cognitive dimensions. This may be done by reference to the passages of Scripture assigned for homework or through material that arises within the session. Choosing whether to make the homework or material within the session the focus will depend upon which lends itself most readily to the accomplishment of the purpose. There must be a smooth flow between the data presented by Joy and Bill in their interaction and the material the pastor brings from his knowledge in dealing with the agenda that was established in the first session. There is a specific teaching role in pastoral counseling because of our commitment and the explicit commitment of the counselee(s) to the Christian perspective presented in the biblical data. We do not apologize for introducing the Christian content and recognize that the expectation is that the pastor will do so. In carefully prethinking and planning the direction of the session in response to where the couple have indicated they are coming from in previous sessions and from the pastor's awareness of data relevant to the area of focus, the pastor has a tentative agenda for the session.

Receiving the Counselees

At the time for the session, the pastor may go to the reception area to receive Joy and Bill. It is our preference to greet persons in the reception area and to bring them into the office, rather than having them ushered in by a secretary or receptionist. This may seem like a small point. However, we interpret our greeting of them as an extension of hospitality, an extension of our hand in friendship and fellowship to them. Henri Nouwen (1975) has a very helpful discussion of hospitality. He suggests that hospitality is creating a free and friendly space. "Hospitality, therefore, means primarily the creation of a free space where the stranger can enter and become a friend instead of an enemy. Hospitality is not to change people, but to offer them space where change can take place" (p. 51).

Pastoral counseling is the hard and intense work of creating that space for growth and providing guidance to focus on the issues in such a manner as to facilitate the person's pursuit of growth. We remove ourselves from the business of other pastoral responsibility to focus our attention and theirs on the issue at hand. If the pastor is distracted, the counselee(s) will also be distracted into the diffusion and lack of clarity that hinders growth. In extending hospitality, we are bringing them into "our territory," and we wish to set aside any nonproductive feelings they may have about being there by warmly welcoming them with courtesy. The formality of such an action expresses a warmth and is, in fact, less formal than the experience we may have in being ushered into a doctor's or dentist's office where we feel we are coming into a professional presence for examination. One needs to consider the process that is involved in getting to the office and the impact of that upon the persons involved. This may mean considering how public the entrance to the pastor's office is and how many people or people's offices must be passed to get to the pastor.

The physical layout of the office may also communicate volumes about the pastor's understanding of the relationship. Lighting, the arrangement of the chairs, visual distractions through windows or doors, audio distractions, and even unusual artifacts in the room may be disruptive. Our preference is for a simple, but comfortable room, without a large desk, extensive library, or other items that may be distracting. The potential for some physical distancing or sitting indirectly, rather than knee to knee, may also be important. The physical environment impacts what happens in the counseling context.

Connecting with Session 2

Pastor: I'm glad to see the two of you today. Bill, you mentioned on Sunday that Joy was home with Jeremy who was not feeling well. Is he well now?

Joy: Thanks for your concern. Yes, he is OK. It was just one of those passing childhood things. I felt bad about missing Sunday school and church, but that's part of being a mother.

Pastor: Well, I'm glad to hear he's well again. Let me review and recap last week's session. The two of you worked very hard at getting in touch with your own and with each other's experience of anger, especially in terms of the feelings we experience associated with anger. Sometimes our feelings are heavy burdens. It is good to share those with each other and to give each other the freedom to do so in an accepting environment. We looked at the matter of acknowledging and accepting our anger while recognizing that acceptance is different than approval. I appreciate your courage in doing that as we work together to understand and develop a strategy to be more effective in dealing with anger. Today, I wonder if we could look at another piece of the puzzle. In the homework we discussed at the end of our time together last week, you were going to continue your journaling with respect to your occasions of anger with special focus on your thought processes in terms of what you thought about yourself or each other and the meaning you may have attributed to the other. In addition, you were going to look at a couple of passages of Scripture. Perhaps, each of you could share briefly what stood out most for you in thinking through what may have been a difficult assignment.

The pastor, here, seeks to be sensitive to experiences outside the counseling session, but not to be distracted by them. In this case, the illness of a child provided a possible distraction. Acknowledging that reality is adequate as a sensitive response, but moving on to the matter at hand is then possible. He then affirms them in what they did and learned in the previous session. The sharing of burdens is an implicit reference to biblical truth to which most church attendees would give assent. It is not necessary to "proof text" every reference to biblical data. This comment affirms their commitment to working at their relationship and acknowledges that what they are doing is not easy. Sometimes working at these personal areas of tension is far more difficult for people than we acknowledge. Leaving it open for either to respond may help to further understand the dynamics between them.

Feelings and Thoughts

Bill: It seems funny to me, but I'm not sure I could distinguish between what I felt and what I thought. For example, the passage I read was about the spies. But I went on to the next chapter and read about the anger of the people toward Moses and Aaron and how they wanted to stone them. Talk about anger!

Pastor: Bill, you have put your finger on a key problem. How do we distinguish between what we feel and what we think? What is the relationship between the two? We can add another dimension to the question as well. What about our behavior? Do we behave as a result of what we feel or what we think, and where does our physical energy to behave aggressively come from or fit into all of this? We are moving very fast at this point. We have to slow the process down and look at the different parts or aspects of anger. We can talk about feelings, thoughts, behavior, and physical dimensions of anger. We must be careful not to jumble it all. So, let's look at one piece at a time. However, we will get to it all.

It would be easy to get sidetracked at this point. Pastors may feel a sermon coming on about the relationship that existed between Moses (and Aaron) and the children of Israel. Inclinations to preach must be resisted. Out of what Bill says, it is important to choose that which will further the purpose to which these sessions are dedicated. An overview that acknowledges the multiplicity of factors may satisfy at this point. The most important place to focus here may be on the confusion between feelings and thoughts.

Joy: I have trouble seeing all these things in anger, also. I see Bill's agitation and I feel hurt when he withdraws. I'd just like us to have some improvement in our relationship, but I guess I'd like a better relationship with the children as well. My home was a peaceful place.

Pastor: Bill, it appears that Joy's comment unsettled you. Can you share which part made you uncomfortable?

It is very important to use the experiences, behavior, thoughts, gestures, body language, and so on that are apparent in the session to further the purpose of the session. However, in some cases you may choose only to acknowledge what has transpired as a means of forestalling it from distracting from the session rather than dealing with it. We would choose to focus on Bill's response at this point only if it is sufficiently evident that without acknowledgment it would detract from the process. In this case, the pastor felt that he had lost Bill because of his reaction to Joy's comment and, therefore, felt his reaction had to be dealt with and made explicit so that it could either be dealt with or they could move beyond it.

> *Bill:* Well, ah . . . I guess I could. I get tired of our family always being badly compared to her family. It's just not the same! *(stated with tentativeness, but strong affect)*
>
> *Pastor:* This comparison really ticks you off, or, to be blunt, angers you. However, you don't at all feel comfortable in saying so. You don't feel safe to say so and, so, it's easier for you to withdraw. Joy, I see that you would like to respond to what Bill has said. Let me ask you to hold your comment for a minute while we understand what is transpiring here. This may illustrate the very issue we need to address.

The pastor is in a bit of a bind here. The intention was to deal with the difference between feeling and thought. However, very heavy feelings and what appears to be a very relevant issue has come up. Do we go with the direction consistent with our overall plan or deal with the existential issue? Or, alternatively, can we use this situation to bring the question of feelings and cognitions into focus? It is wise to respond to the strong desire Joy evidences to defend herself. However, it is helpful also to introduce the discipline of pursuing understanding before we express what may be just more affect without the understanding that may come from thoughtful exploration. It is the pastor's responsibility to guide the process.

> *Pastor:* Let's look at Joy's comment that provided the stimulus for Bill's reaction. You first acknowledged, Joy, that you

did not understand the several dimensions of anger that I had identified, that is, feeling, thinking, physical energy, and behavior. Then, you said you see Bill's agitation. That is your perception of his feeling, which is evidenced by body language, which is a form of behavior, which expresses feeling and is, at least partly, a result of the physiology of anger. You, then, said you felt hurt, which is your feeling, and that Bill withdraws, which is descriptive of his behavior as you see it. You moved from there to talk of your desire for peace in your relationship with both Bill and the children. When you speak of your home as a peaceful place, you sound wistful and are expressing an evaluation of the experience you had there, which contrasts with your present experience. You have, in fact, touched on all the elements that I suggested are involved in the experience of anger. You focused on Bill's behavior and physiological manifestation of anger, your feelings, the feelings you attributed to Bill, and your cognitive processing which leads to some comparative analyses. If we could explore your thoughts, evaluations, and reasoning as you direct them toward yourself and Bill, we would then have a fairly complete picture. Before we explore that any further, let me see if we can get in touch with Bill's response. Bill's discomfort and agitation were obvious and, I expect, Joy, you were aware of that. Bill, I wonder if you could help us understand what you experienced. It will be helpful if you can share your feelings in terms of your emotions, as well as any physical sensations you experienced.

The choice here was to focus on Joy's comment to formulate a different perspective that was accepting and explorative, while at the same time directing attention to a different perspective from which to understand her response. Developing an alternative perspective, which has greater potential for more accurate understanding and more effective coping, is the goal. The pastor chooses to focus on Joy because of the depth of Bill's affective response, thus attempting to make it safe for him and creating some space for him to process what he experienced in the terms used to describe Joy's response. It is often easier for a person to learn in the role of an observer than as the one who is receiving primary attention. At this point, it is assumed Bill is ready to look at his own reaction.

Feelings and the Family Tree

Bill: I don't know if I was aware of any physical sensations, but I sure experienced a surge of anger and the feeling of being judged.

Pastor: Let's explore this "surge" you experienced. Where in your body was it experienced?

Bill: Well, I kind of felt a bloating in my stomach and pressure in my throat, but I was more conscious of my feeling judged.

Pastor: True, we are often not as conscious of bodily sensations as we are of feelings. We need to come back to these bodily sensations. However, let's look at the "feeling judged" for a moment. How do you feel when judged? Do you feel inadequate, little, shamed, guilty, that you don't measure up, or all of the above?

Bill: Well, I sure feel I don't measure up and, I guess, I feel like a kid rather than an adult.

Pastor: That sounds a bit like the feelings of a biblical character you may know. Do you remember Jeremiah? When God called him to be a prophet he responded, "Ah, Sovereign LORD, I do not know how to speak; I am only a child" (Jer. 1:6). Or maybe you remember the observation of the spies that you read about in Numbers 13. They said, "We seemed like grasshoppers in our own eyes." Your response to what Joy said was to think of yourself as a child or a grasshopper. Notice, I said, "You think of yourself as a child or as a grasshopper." You said, "I feel like a kid rather than an adult." This may help us to understand the difference between feeling and thinking. When you think of yourself as a child, which you know not to be the case, you feel belittled, small, inadequate, that you do not measure up, and so on. It is true that feelings influence thinking, and it is also true that thinking influences feelings. In fact, we could add that attitudes influence behavior and behavior influences attitudes. It appears that anger seeps into our experience through several gateways including feeling, thinking, behavior, and physiology. Do you mind if I encourage you to explore this a bit more?

Bill: No, I think I'm beginning to get the drift.

Pastor: Let's bring in another factor. Not only anger, but feelings, thoughts, and behavior patterns are the fruits that grow in family trees. Do you have any recollection of being called or accused of being a child, a baby, or in some way being belittled as you were growing up?

Bill: Oh, sure. My older brother was unmerciful in teasing me about being "the baby" or of behaving like a child even when I was in my early teens. Come to think of it, my mother always compared me unfavorably to older siblings. Boy, did that tick me off!

Pastor: It would be fair to say, then, that you learned to respond to such belittling with the response of anger. And, you developed a sensitivity to such name calling or being minimized. Such a sensitivity, then, only requires a trigger to activate the response of anger or of the thinking process which attributes to one's self the appraisal "I am a child" or "I am being appraised as being a child." In a sense, that trigger puts us on autopilot, which activates a sequence of thoughts, feelings, and behavior, which is accompanied by physiological responses in our body which, in effect, energize us for action. Now, this brings us to another crucial question: Where does the appraisal that "I am a child" come from? We feel accused. But where is the source of the accusation? Let's go back to our two biblical examples. Where did Jeremiah's appraisal that he was a child come from? Did God think of him as a child?

Joy: The answer to that is, "No."

Pastor: Right, in verse 7 it says, "Do not say, 'I am only a child.'" God had declared earlier that he had formed Jeremiah in the womb, set him apart, and appointed him to be a prophet. Certainly, God did not think him to be a child. Similarly, the spies who concluded they were grasshoppers in their own eyes had no basis for believing the giants in the land thought them to be grasshoppers. However, they rationalized, "We looked the same to them" (Num. 13:33). This is what we commonly call projection. Projection is where one person projects on another a perception or conclusion that they have reached concerning themselves, which may be negative or positive. In the case of the spies, they thought of themselves as grasshoppers, inadequate, incapable, and of lesser ability than the giants, and then projected that picture of themselves onto the giants, concluding that the giants thought them to be grasshoppers. The response of the Israelites was a subjective response informed by their feelings about themselves. Jeremiah was expressing his subjective feeling in the thought, "I am a child."

Bill: I guess I can identify with the spies in that.

Pastor: You know, Bill, we can often learn about ourselves by looking at the experience of others. Often the subjective response is related to personal pain that is unresolved and is carried in our mental attitude toward ourselves. Another way to express this is to acknowledge that all experience is informed by previous experience. One may question whether our response is more informed by the past than by the present situation. When our response is reflexive, it often has much to do with the subjective elements we bring to the situation. I wonder, Bill, if this has any application to your thinking process. Joy provides a trigger. You respond on automatic pilot with thoughts and feelings associated with those feelings from the past and associate them with feelings that you are being deemed less or small or inadequate as compared to Joy's family. Do you see any possibility that this process could be operative here?

Bill: I suppose, but she did make the comparison.

Pastor: Let's check that out. She said she saw your agitation and withdrawal and felt hurt. She then went on to express a desire for peace, which you have indicated you share. She then identified her home as a place where such peace was experienced. She sounded kind of wistful to me at that point. Could we check with Joy to see if she intended accusation, belittling, or if she perceives you to be a child?

Joy: I long for peace, probably because I don't know how to handle conflict and anger. I sure don't see Bill as a child; I just don't understand his anger, or my own either, I guess. I really have no desire to accuse Bill; I really appreciate so much about him. However, I do get frustrated.

Pastor: Well, peace may not be best defined as the absence of conflict or anger. Perhaps, we need to see conflict and anger as a pathway to peace as long as we can experience these in safety and in a way that leads to growth and understanding. Joy, in my comment to you a minute ago, I introduced another important consideration. I asked about your intention. It is important to see that our intentions are often not well expressed in our words or our behavior and, for this reason, are not as obvious to another person as we think they should be. Let me expand this a little. Your intentions, which you now express as a desire for peace in your relationships, were not explicit in what you said. Is that a fair statement?

Joy: I think so. I guess I said I wanted improvement. I didn't even consciously compare our family and my parents' family. The idea of peace is important to me.

Pastor: Bill certainly didn't hear that intention, but, of course, his response was fueled by unresolved issues, those subjective factors, from his feeling belittled by his brother and mother. I am not interested in the issue of who is to blame for this mix-up in communication. Blame may be irrelevant and impossible to assess. Bill, if Joy had said a while ago, "I would value peace in our relationships in our family, such as we sometimes have, probably because I experienced peace in my family of origin," do you think you would have responded in the same way?

Bill: It is hard to say, but I could say, "I want peace, too." We agree on that! I guess I know she experienced peace in her family. The way you put it sounds softer.

Pastor: That's the key. You say you could agree on that. That's because that statement expresses a desire, intention, or value, that is, peace. Also, the word "probably" brings a tentativeness to the statement about Joy's family and makes it softer. You would not feel judged or criticized in the same way. Your "trigger" would not be pulled. Really, we have identified two issues. One, how we express ourselves is crucial. We need to learn to express intention and to express ourselves with tentativeness which avoids criticism, judgment, or put-down. Second, the emotional baggage we bring from the past often is triggered to activate anger in the present. Therefore, dealing with some of that emotional baggage which we have incorporated into our thinking patterns like Jeremiah—"I am a child"—or the Israelites—"We became like grasshoppers in our own sight"—is important so that we do not respond on automatic pilot to triggers activated by others.

Bill: That makes sense to me. We are both involved in this process, so I guess we can work at it together.

Pride and Humility

Pastor: There is another aspect to this that I would like to introduce. We are concerned about effectiveness in communicating and effectiveness in dealing with differences and our expression of anger. To be effective in communication we have to deal with our need to be right, to have our perceptions affirmed, and to be approved in our opinions. Our need to be right focuses on our perspective, making it the center of our understanding. The biblical term for that is pride. Pride absolutizes our personal perspective, declaring it right. In communication, this means we insist on our perspective as the only valid one. Pride prefers one's own dogma without the confusion that occurs when another's perspective is given careful consideration. One writer speaks of "the ever-reforming spirit of humility" (Myers, 1996). In contrast to pride, humility seeks to enter into the other's experience through the pursuit of understanding and thoughtful consideration of the other's perspective. Humility is the expression of a self secure in an identity that is willing and open to consider the perspective of others without denying one's own perspective. Putting it very simply, pride is defensive and humility is openness. In pride, we insulate ourselves by withdrawing into our self-defined world or by attacking what is different and, in essence, declaring what is different is wrong and we are right. Humility seeks the other's perspective, not to yield, but to understand, to consider, to evaluate, and in doing so to honor and to benefit from that different perspective and to incorporate truth into our own perspective. Great care must be taken to not assume that we understand the other's intention, and to express our own intention. The attribution of intention usually gets us into trouble. Learning to make our intentions explicit is most important in communicating clearly. Joy, do you see how your expression of your intention in an overt or explicit way would have helped in this communication with Bill?

Joy: Well, yes, I guess I just assumed he would know my intention and that's probably not a fair assumption. I just had no idea that what I said would trigger his feeling from his family. I didn't even know how he felt in his family.

Pastor: That's understandable. Bill was unaware of the association of past feelings with the trigger also. Let's develop this a little further. When you withdraw, Bill, and play that little tape that says, "I am a child," or "I am not measuring up," you experience anger toward yourself, which I call imploding, that is, turning inward with self-negation or self-harm. When you act outwardly toward Joy, you are exploding, that is, turning your anger toward another or toward something outside yourself. Let me encourage you to read about these two ways of expressing anger in the book you are reading together as we work through these sessions. I think we have enough time left for me to introduce another way of looking at anger which will help you greatly. I call this the anger equation. Let me begin by saying that anger is not really the problem. God experiences anger. Being created in his image, it is not surprising that we experience similar emotions. We are most conscious of anger as emotion. However, it is a physiological response as well. *(At this point, we would draw a diagram.)*

Joy: That diagram makes it much clearer to me.

Pastor: Perhaps we do not need to elaborate the emotional side of anger. We often do not have as clear an understanding of the physiological aspects of anger. Put simply, anger is an energizing of the body. It is accomplished through our autonomic nervous system, which elevates heart rate and blood pressure, redistributes the blood to large muscle systems and to the surface of the body, and brings about many other changes. The result is that we are energized for action. It is for this reason that if we physically hit another in anger, the force is much greater than we intend. The foot-pounds of energy are much greater than a similar striking would be if not expressed in anger. The force of our actions is much, much greater when those actions are taken in anger. It is for this reason that anger frightens us so much. Both the emotions and the physiology of anger, when expressed often, cause great harm either to self or others. If imploded, anger can lead us to hurt ourselves physically, emotionally, or spiritually by things we think or do. However, if we explode with anger toward others, great harm can come also. Many of us opt for expressing anger inward rather than risking the danger of exploding toward others. When we do so, we often become our own worst enemy. The war no one wins is the war we have with ourselves. The experience of anger may express itself in emotional expression in feelings, thoughts, or behavior, which may be directed inward or outward, imploding or exploding. This is why anger frightens us so much. It often leads to destructive outcomes.

Bill: I have never looked at it quite that way, but it helps me understand why I get frightened by my own anger, as well as that of others.

Pastor: Let me suggest that we turn from the expression of anger to another direction at this point. Put the issues of expression in abeyance for a few minutes. Let's consider where the anger comes from: what provokes anger? where does it begin? This may be a little oversimplified, but it will give us some handles so that we may understand our anger better. Let me ask you a question. What provoked God's anger toward the children of Israel when they were coming out of Egypt?

Joy: They didn't believe he could deliver them and they didn't obey his commandments.

Bill: They didn't accept the leadership of Moses, whom God appointed. Also, they made the calf and worshiped it. God became really ticked off about that!

Pastor: Right. Now let me suggest that God's commandments are an expression of what he values, that is, what is important to him. He expected these people to accept the leadership he appointed and, I am sure, he expected gratitude for his abundant provision for them. Also, he said they were not to create an image or idol as a representation of him. He is devalued by any comparison to any created thing. Now, we have here four things that anger God: (1) He is angered when his goals are not met, (2) he is angered when his values are breached, (3) he is angered when his expectations are breached, and (4) he is angered when his self, or sense of worth, is breached by representation in an idol. It is my observation that we become angry in response to the same things. When I experience a breach of my values, a breach of my expectations, or a breach of my sense of worth, then I become angry. Obviously, when God becomes angry, he can express himself without sin. When I become angry, I have difficulty expressing myself without sin. Paul says, "Be angry, but do not sin." He seems to imply that it is possible to avoid sin in experiencing anger. Anger may be one of the good gifts God has given us if we can move from our acknowledgment of anger backward to understand whether it has been activated by a breach of our goals, values, expectations, or sense of worth. If we can identify these, we can talk meaningfully about them. With this equation in mind, let's go back to our discussion earlier in this session. Joy, what was the value you were suggesting earlier that was important in your experience in your family?

Joy: Peace. That was important to me.

Pastor: Right. And, if we took time to explore what peace means to you, we would understand how important it is and what it means to you. But let's hold that for a minute. Often, we know our values only if we explore our response when they are breached. In our reaction we can often understand what is breached and that is often the opposite of what we have experienced. For example, Bill, you responded to Joy's original comment by feeling compared and by activating thoughts related to being a child and not measuring up. What value of yours would be breached at that point?

Bill: Well, I guess my sense of worth . . . but also I feel unaccepted, so, I guess, my value of being accepted. In fact, I guess that's what I experience at work, too. I don't know if I measure up, or if I'm accepted and valued. I feel pretty insecure in both places.

Pastor: You'd really like acceptance, security, and to be valued.

Bill: I sure would. I don't know that I ever felt really valued.

Pastor: Can we add, Bill, that when your sense of worth is breached, you feel your security and acceptance, which you value highly, are breached and that you become angry?

Bill: I guess that's clear enough.

Pastor: Bill, you have shown courage in exploring these issues. Let me say, your anger is very appropriate. In fact, God joins you in anger when your worth is breached and he wants you to be secure and to experience acceptance. Your worth, acceptance, and security with him is beyond question. What you want is the same thing in relation to others. Can we bring this discussion back to the relationship between you and Joy?

Bringing Closure

The pastor has been observing Joy's response to all of this. She has appeared surprised, puzzled, and sad as Bill has been exploring these issues. It is important to bring them to some sense of direction as the time to conclude the session is approaching. It is important to deal with the deep emotion Bill has experienced, but to also enable Joy to process her experience. Also, it may be important to note here the possible need to follow up or refer Bill to deal with the issues revealed. However, the purpose of this counseling program must not be forgotten. We need to come back to the relationship between Bill and Joy and the application of what has been learned to that relationship.

Pastor: Joy, I've been very conscious of your response to what Bill has grappled with and realize you have had a mix of emotions. Do you feel you could share with us your experience and understanding?

Joy: I have had all kinds of feelings and thoughts. I had no idea this was how Bill felt. I want him to be secure with me and I see him as very worthy. I saw him as strong and even aggressive. Maybe I interpreted his anger as strength. I didn't know my comparisons meant that to him. I feel awful and confused.

Pastor: Joy, your love for Bill is clear. Perhaps, Bill didn't understand his anger any better than you did. When we are taught to deny anger or to turn it inward or to cover it in some way, we don't understand it and others don't either. We can move toward reducing the confusion when we, first, acknowledge and accept our anger; second, decide to hold action or thoughts in abeyance; third, ask whether goals, values, expectations, or sense of worth have been breached; and, fourth, communicate in terms of our goals, values, expectations, or sense of worth. Until both Bill and you know the source of the anger that is triggered by your comment, neither of you will understand his expression of anger. It will be confusing to both of you. Perhaps, this is what you are responding to when you say, "I had no idea this was how Bill felt."

Joy: I certainly experience the confusion. Obviously, when we relate at the level of action and reaction without knowing what is behind that, we aren't communicating clearly or effectively. We need to know where we are each coming from.

Pastor: You have expressed that well. Let me see if I can briefly summarize what we have learned in this time together. Anger often activates a reflexive response that is like being on automatic pilot. The trigger that activates the anger is in the immediate. The reflexive response is energized by subjective elements that may be related to unresolved pain from the past. If we act out of that subjectively informed anger, our feelings, thoughts, and actions will not be an appropriate response to the immediate, but rather a response to the past. This leads to harm either to self or to others. Thus I need to put that response in abeyance and cognitively assess whether my present experience is a response to a breach of goals, values, expectations, or my sense of worth. If I understand this, I may then free myself from the focus on me to focus on the other's intention. This is what we talked about earlier as a shift from pride to humility, by seeking to understand what the other is experiencing. Knowing that my values were breached, I can rationally discuss this with the person to compare values and to clarify their intention toward me. We recognized, also, that if we expressed our intention overtly to the other, we would be less likely to elicit an anger response.

Bill: If my anger has more to do with values, expectations, and self-worth, which is fueled by past experience, then Joy's immediate comment, the trigger, needs to be understood differently.

Pastor: That is exactly true, Bill. Also, if I deal with the past hurts that are energizing my subjective, reflexive response, I would free myself from that effect. Dealing with pain from the past, communicating intention, and cognitively understanding what evokes anger will help greatly in enabling us to deal with anger more effectively. Putting this another way, freeing myself from a conditioned response so that I may make a considered response based upon thoughtful assessment while I, with humility, seek to understand the other's perspective is a big step in the right direction. Wow! We have covered a great deal today! I wonder if each of you could share one thing that you feel you've picked up from this rather heavy session.

It is often helpful to have the counselees summarize what was for them the most important learning. This can be informative for the pastor and helpful in fixing in their minds some significant learning. The Spirit of God is at work in making relevant in the sessions what is of specific importance to the individuals. What they focus on may be a clue to some other issues that may need to be dealt with. This request for their sharing is best done in a nondemanding way to lessen the possibility that they feel they have to perform or have to express appreciation.

Bill: Well, I feel mentally drained. I guess most surprising for me was the realization that my anger may have more to do with my past than the trigger that Joy or others provide for me in the present. You talked of anger as a gift. I certainly never saw it that way. It makes sense that my anger could point to what is important to me. I guess that's the sense in which it is a gift. I have a lot of thinking to do about all of this.

Pastor: That's a good summary, Bill, and it is hard work. When you speak of your anger as a gift, I would like to say it is a gift to the other person when you share with them what is very important to you. Only that way can they know you. Joy, do you feel comfortable in concluding at this point?

Joy: Yes, this has been heavy, but I've learned some things. I've tended to focus on Bill's anger without understanding it. I've never thought of expressing my intentions and, instead, jump to conclusions. I have been wondering if the reason I was never very conscious of anger in my family was because my values were never challenged and my sense of worth was not an issue. In fact, I guess I was never compared. I need to look at my anger toward the kids in terms of their breaching my goals, expectations, values, or sense of worth.

Homework

Pastor: The courage to explore and to seek understanding always leads to more adventure in growth. Let me suggest some homework for next week. I would like you to both reflect on an incident of anger this week. Spend some time together listing your feelings, thoughts, and the way you expressed the anger. Use some of the things that we have discussed today. Second, we would like to look at the relationship between anger and justice, vengeance and forgiveness as we explore this further. Read Romans 12:17–21 and Luke 17:1–10 and reflect on how these Scriptures may apply to your marriage and to your relationships in general.

6

VENGEANCE AND FORGIVENESS
SESSION 4

Summary: This session moves more into the behavioral dimensions of anger with a particular focus on the relationship between hurt, vengeance, and forgiveness. When experiencing this level of anger, we will choose behavioral responses that are characterized by passivity, aggressiveness, or assertiveness. Key to the selection of the appropriate response is our commitment to freedom, worth, and community.

Unfinished Business

Pastor: I sensed that we dealt with some important material in our last time together and I wondered how you both processed it.

Joy (with a smile): We had a big fight!

Bill: We did not have to wait too long after the session to do the first part of our homework. We were both steaming at each other within no time.

Pastor: Well, let's start with that situation tonight. Can you give me a sense of what happened?

Counseling sessions can start in any number of ways. Sometimes people will jump into a description of a situation, like Joy, and provide the pastor with the opportunity to simply follow their direction. In the current situation, the pastor did not have to do too much work to get things started, except to simply respond empathically. At other times people will come to counseling with more present and immediate needs that may have been precipitated by the ride to the office or a conversation in the waiting room. As a co-pilgrim in the counseling process, the pastor needs to be sensitive to the parishioner's state and not feel the need to determine direction in every situation.

Bill: Towards the end of our last session I recognized, again, that one of our major problems is Joy's difficulty in being at home with Jeremy and Shannon. The first seven years we were married she had a middle-management position in a retail store and she found a lot of fulfillment, personally and professionally. Since Jeremy was born she has been at home, although she had hoped she would go back to work when he went to school full time, but then Shannon came along.

Joy: That is exactly where the problem comes in. I had hoped to go back to work, but Bill was not supportive. He thought I should be content at home, looking after children, making meals, and attending to his every need. I have tried to be industrious and creative at home, but I have felt the lack of professional contact and fulfillment that comes from working outside the home. Bill does not understand this.

Bill: I understand it. I just don't agree with it.

Pastor: You indicated that this situation last week tied in to the first part of your homework. I had suggested that you take an incident and note the feelings, thoughts, and expression of anger. Did you have a chance to process what happened using these terms?

This is an excellent intervention by the pastor. When people begin to relay stories, it is easy for them and for the counselor to get lost in the details of the story and not focus on the underlying goal. This is particularly true in short-term strategic counseling where there is no time to pursue stories in great detail. The story is important, though, and the pastor has wisely brought Bill back to his earlier comment and invited him to link the incident with the homework. The pastor communicates the importance of reframing incidents in language that will be helpful and facilitative of growth. To simply recount stories in a marriage will produce minimal change. However, when the stories are relayed by employing concepts like feelings, thoughts, and expression, the anger will be better understood.

Hurt and Vengeance

Joy: I am finding it hard to deal with Bill's description of the issue now that we are in your office. He says that I have difficulty being at home, but he does not talk about his anger and his demands that I have to put up with when we discuss this privately. He has even started trotting out biblical passages to substantiate his arguments. This makes me feel resentful and frustrated.

Pastor: I sense that we are starting to dissect this problem in a little more detail. Bill, what about you? What kinds of feelings do you experience around Joy's struggle with being at home?

Bill: I don't know what to say about this in light of what you told us the last time. You talked about pride being the absolutizing of our personal perspective and I am wondering whether this is happening for me.

Pastor: Let's address that shortly, but let me encourage you to focus on the feelings. What do you experience when this issue comes up between you and Joy?

Joy has indicated that Bill is being more placid in the counseling situation than he normally is. This response is not uncharacteristic of people in counseling. It is sometimes easier to talk about the cognitive side of the problem and bypass the emotive component. Bill is avoiding the "feeling" question by moving into the discussion of pride that occurred in the last session. The pastor, wisely, brings him back and indicates that the feeling side needs to be dealt with first.

Bill (frustrated): Well, if I have to talk about it, then I will. I am sick and tired of Joy's lack of contentment in the home. At this stage it is about employment and being a homemaker, but before that it was spending time with friends and visiting her family. She never wants to stay home and that makes me mad. Is there something wrong with the home? Is there something wrong with me? Is the apostle Paul wrong when he says that women should be at home and not outside the home? I am so ticked with all this, I hardly know what to say.

Joy: When I hear this, I feel really sad and I feel rejected. It is almost as if Bill is negating who I am and what is important to me. More often than not, the sadness and rejection moves into anger and I want to get back at him because of what he is doing to me.

Pastor: As we have talked about the last few weeks, it is important to get the feelings out on the table so you know what you are dealing with. It is clear that you are angry at each other and I sense a vengeful, almost hurtful, response toward each other. Do you have any understanding of the thoughts that are lurking behind these feelings?

Bill: I found our last session helpful and I have been trying to look at the link between feelings and thoughts, but I am a little stumped. Can you give me some ways to help make this link?

These kinds of questions can easily lead to simple answers. However, the pastor needs to stay with the material that has been provided by Bill. Linking feelings and thoughts is not achieved by a simple formula. There are no ten-step programs to answer this question. What has Bill communicated already? In the last session, he described a family environment where he felt belittled and put down. This may have produced a level of insecurity and discomfort, which, in turn, has led him to respond to Joy as a trigger to that insecurity. This, in turn, produces anger. One of the questions he has asked rhetorically in this session is interesting: "Is there something wrong with me?" It would appear that Bill is personalizing Joy's absence. This speculation is worth checking out.

> *Pastor:* When we are trying to figure out the thinking process of our anger, we need to take our focus off the event that seems to have produced the irritation. We need to look at ourselves and ask some questions about what is going on inside of us. Bill, you will remember in our last session we talked about your feelings of being deemed inadequate compared to Joy's family. A few minutes ago you asked the question: "Is there something wrong with me?" I sense that Joy's absence, whether it be for work or to be with friends, makes you feel something. Can you put that into words?
>
> *Bill:* I don't know. I feel sort of . . . well, it is sort of silly, I guess . . . I feel insecure almost to the point of feeling like she does not want to be with me.
>
> *Pastor:* Can you finish this sentence for me, Bill? I will be secure and significant if Joy. . . .

The pastor has done a good job of gently presenting some material from the last session and the current session. This is a confrontation of the best kind. Bill is being confronted by Bill. The pastor has not exposed Bill in a way that strips the layers off insensitively. He has simply moved him toward a new insight that will be helpful for future conflicts. Notice also that the focus is on having Bill deal with Bill, rather than with Joy. The pastor is not focusing on the stimuli that seemed to produce the anger, but is inviting Bill into some healthy self-examination. In sum, Bill is not being forced to deal with the power of the pastor or the behavior of Joy.

The unfinished sentence is an extremely helpful way of moving parishioners into an understanding of their own identity. In the presence of others' behavior we find our sense of security and significance is impacted. When a teenage boy is dumped by his girlfriend, he can feel rejected, negated, even devalued. Why does this happen? Because his identity has been impacted by others' behavior. What others do to us often reveals how we feel and what we think about ourselves. When a fifty-year-old woman loses her job after giving twenty years to the company, her identity may be impacted. She may feel useless, incompetent, even insignificant. Her personal security and significance are revealed through the circumstantial event.

When Bill gets angry because Joy wants to spend time with friends or have a career, it would be easy for the pastor to analyze Joy's behavior. Is it appropriate for her to have friends or a career? Should she be pursuing these ventures? On the other hand, the intensity of Bill's anger requires that his response be understood. Only then can the two of them have a clear understanding of the real reason for Bill's intense anger. The alternative is for Bill's anger to create an environment where everyone, including Joy, needs to change their behavior so he experiences no discomfort.

Bill: I will be secure and significant if Joy is around all the time.

Pastor: Can you repeat the first half of the sentence and tell me all the phrases that come to mind when you think of Joy's friends and career.

Bill: I will be secure and significant if I am the only focus in Joy's life. I will be secure and significant if she caters to all my needs. I will be secure and significant if other parts of Joy's life do not compete with her relationship with me. I will be secure and significant if Joy lets me. . . . I don't want to go any further with this.

Pastor: Why is that?

Bill: I don't like what I am saying. It seems that my security and significance are tied up in my relationship with Joy to such an extreme that I cannot bear to have her develop her own life. It feels like we are back to the stuff we talked about last session. You know, my sense of being put down at home.

Pastor: You have been very honest about your thinking. It seems that Joy's absence triggers a deep feeling of insecurity inside you which, in turn, precipitates anger. That is quite a normal link. Sometimes we cope with our hurt by reacting with anger. What we are talking about right now is very important for both of you. To understand that our hurt and anger may be triggered by someone else's behavior, but not necessarily caused by it, is an important awareness.

Joy: That's an important distinction that I have never thought of.

Pastor: I remember a fellow who used to go to the church a number of years ago. Any time things did not happen the way he wanted them to, he would get very upset and hostile. He would confront me and the rest of the leadership and often lash out at other members. In spite of many conversations over these issues, he could not get past the fact that others were making him mad. He held them totally and absolutely responsible. He could not see the link between others' behavior and his hurt, anger, and behavioral outbursts. Sadly, he left the church and went to another fellowship where the same thing happened. He was continually angry with what others were doing, but he could not see where he was contributing to the intensity of the reaction.

Bill: As you said in the last session, it takes some humility to get to that point and most of us do not specialize in that area! I guess, if I am honest, I tend to only use the Scriptures in this area when I am being proud, not when I am being humble. When Joy leaves the home and I feel insecure, I cast about to find something to throw at her. I know that Scripture is important to her so I talk about the biblical message that women should stay in the home. To be honest, I have never studied that issue and I don't even know if the Bible teaches it or not.

When Christians get angry, they can often use the spiritual mask of legalism, rigidity, and criticism. They may quote Scripture or use biblical language to buttress their argument, but at the core they are simply angry and looking for a way to support their position. Bill has the humility to admit that his use of Scripture fits into this category. The Bible is not given as a support to our personal grievances, but as an expression of God's truth spoken into our current difficulties. Clearly, in this case, Bill does not need biblical exegesis on the role of women in the workplace. He needs to drop this layer and see himself for what he is. This approach allows him to be less defensive and to focus more on self-understanding and exploration.

Joy: I think what is hard for me in Bill's reaction is that it is quite vengeful. I get the sense that he wants to get back at me and even the score. This is quite overwhelming. In fact, I think both of us react this way at times. The Romans 12 homework really addressed that quite specifically.

Pastor: I am interested in the way you have understood the Romans 12 passage. Let me read it with you and then you can tell me more about your understanding.

Do not repay anyone evil for evil. Be careful to do what is right in the eyes of everybody. If it is possible, as far as it depends on you, live at peace with everyone. Do not take revenge, my friends, but leave room for God's wrath, for it is written: "It is mine to avenge; I will repay," says the Lord. On the contrary: "If your enemy is hungry, feed him; if he is thirsty, give him something to drink. In doing this, you will heap burning coals on his head." Do not be overcome by evil, but overcome evil with good. (vv. 17–21)

Joy: What struck me was our natural tendency to react to evil with evil. The whole section speaks against what comes easy for us. When someone does something wrong we want to get back at them. I guess that is how I see justice—an evening of the score. In fact, when Bill starts going on about his lack of tolerance with Jim at the plant, it reminds me of his intolerance of me, so I start to pick at him and question why he is treating Jim the way he is. Before you know it, I am really letting him have it. But the passage says that I am not to overcome evil with evil but with good. How do I do that?

In response to this question, the pastoral counselor has a decision to make. The expert knowledge orientation would suggest that it is the counselor's responsibility to provide the answers to all the parishioner's questions. The parishioner only needs to come with their questions. This style of counseling pushed to the extreme can create an unhealthy dependence so that the parishioner requires the pastor in order to answer any significant question. The common knowledge orientation would suggest that the answer to the question is resident inside everyone, and Joy should be able to come up with a personal response to her own question. She only needs the pastor to guide and facilitate the process. The extreme of this approach to counseling moves the pastor into a passive role where there is no educating or communication of truth. A divine knowledge orientation recognizes that biblical truth is able to guide people into knowledge and understanding. With this awareness, the pastor would point Joy back to the Scriptures so they can help her understand the process of overcoming evil with good. In order to do that, the pastor must have some understanding of the passage under consideration.

The first sentence in Romans 12:17 makes it clear that the natural tendency to repay evil for evil should not occur in any interpersonal situation (in contrast to the governmental and civil sphere where authorities become "God's servants . . . agents of wrath" [13:4]). How does this happen? By "being careful to do what is right in the eyes of everybody." At first glance this seems like an invitation to be a people pleaser—make sure everyone sees what you are doing. But Paul is arguing for planning ahead. When you are careful to do what is right, you are anticipating situations where difficulties may occur and deciding, in advance, that you will do the right thing. Then others will experience and observe your righteous behavior.

But this is not a guarantee that all relationships will work out well. There will be people who treat us poorly even though we are seeking to do what is right. Verse 18 captures this scenario. The sense of "if it is possible, as far as it depends on you" is that we need to do everything we can to be on proper terms with others. We need to exhaust all avenues in order to be at peace with others. However, this strategy does not necessarily lead to a positive outcome. Who is responsible for peace in a relationship? Both parties. Christians cannot make it their goal to be at peace with everyone, but it is their responsibility to "make every effort to live in peace with all" (Heb. 12:14).

This truth can be tremendously reassuring to people who feel guilty when relationships are not perfect. At times you can go to someone who is struggling with you and ask for forgiveness, or request dialogue, or express a willingness to resolve the problems. In so doing, you are attempting to do all that you can to facilitate peace. You soon realize that not everyone is willing to pursue the avenue of peace. In those cases, your desire for resolution is not met with a mutual response. Reassurance can only come from the realization that you have made every effort.

Paul then returns, in verse 19, to the absolute prohibition regarding vengeance by providing the rationale. Why should we not engage in "pay back" when someone wrongs us? Vengeance belongs to God. It is his prerogative and his responsibility. Since only God can judge human thought and intent with accuracy, he is much better equipped to respond to the evil that others do toward us. For us to take it on ourselves is to rob God of something that he owns: "It is mine to avenge; I will repay." So what is the alternative? Paul addresses this question in verse 20: "On the contrary."

While the Christian is not to even the score with the enemy, he/she is to reach out and minister. If they are hungry, they are to be given food. Drink is to be provided if they are thirsty. The enemy is not responded to in ways that correspond with their evil, but is cared for in terms of their own personal needs. The offended party does not make the enemy responsible horizontally, but commits them to God who will deal with their sin in his own way and time. In a similar fashion, the offended party also becomes accountable to God by ministering to the enemy and giving them what they do not deserve.

This passage provides details on what it means to love others. Jesus had taught the importance of loving your enemies (Matt. 5:44) and Paul now demonstrates that this love is not an emotive response toward the other. Who feels positive toward those who are enemies? If anything, our enemies elicit negative feelings and hostile emotions. But the command to love is oriented more toward our knowledge and our will than our feelings. It is a command that addresses a behavioral ethic—feed him, give him something to drink. In doing this "you will heap burning coals on his head." At first glance, this may seem like a not-so-subtle form of vengeance. Respond to the enemy's needs and you will be able to get him back with burning coals. Obviously, this is not the thrust of the passage, given what has preceded it. There are at least two other potential explanations. In its cultural setting, a pan of coals placed on the head was a public expression of repentance. Explicit deeds of kindness may provoke remorse. On the other hand, if your neighbor's fireplace had gone out, you could bring a burning coal to relight the flame, and in so doing express Christian charity. Behavioral expressions of love could result in either repentance or an experience of kindness.

Verse 21 of this chapter summarizes the argument succinctly. The presence of evil in interpersonal relationships allows for one of two responses—evil or good. The former is the route of vengeance, of evening the score or seeking personal justice. The latter is the path of love, of doing good and expressing kindness. This choice is difficult as the term "overcome" reflects, a term that gives a sense of battle and conquering. But the bottom line is clear. We are not responsible for others' evil toward us, but we are responsible for our response to the evil.

Forgiveness and Vengeance

Joy: I find the discussion about hurt and vengeance to be helpful, but I am wondering about where forgiveness fits in. Is there a connection between vengeance, justice, and forgiveness? I am not sure what it means to forgive. Does forgiving mean forgetting? Does anger remain after forgiveness? I am quite confused how all these issues fit together.

Pastor: I read a little book a number of years ago by David Augsburger (1984) that I found very helpful in this area. I had preached about forgiveness many times but an issue came up in my family that made me realize that I did not understand all the issues involved, at least in a practical way.

The pastor has provided a helpful intervention in a number of different ways. Bill and Joy may want to pick up this book and find some of the information out for themselves. But he has talked about the book in a personal sense. This is not a pastor who has never experienced struggles or difficulties, but one who has preached on the subject of forgiveness and still needed help when he was confronted with a personal problem. Again, the pastor's sense of co-pilgrimage brings validity to what the couple is experiencing and allows all three of them to move together under God. Crucial to this process is the pastor's recognition that cognitive understanding expressed in preaching does not always manifest itself in the practical realm. He shows wisdom when he acknowledges that he was able to speak on a subject, but did not comprehend it at a practical level.

Pastor: Augsburger talks about three important ingredients in forgiveness. The first is understanding the other person. When we are angry with someone, we not only feel like expressing vengeance, we are also short on understanding. In fact, we believe that the other person does not deserve our understanding. One aspect of forgiveness is the ability and the willingness to be understanding of the other person's experience. In doing this, we are not trying to totally understand the other person and dissect all their motives and intents. Rather, we are seeking to recognize that there are reasons behind all our actions and that all of us are not totally made up of negative qualities and actions. So when someone does something that upsets us, we recognize that there may have been reasons for this, and, furthermore, there is more to this person than this one behavior.

Bill: That is such a problem for me when it comes to Joy's discontentment at home. I am just mad she feels this way. Frankly, I am not the least bit interested in trying to understand what she is going through or what she is feeling. I am just ticked that she is not happy being at home. I suppose I also fall into the other trap as well. Sometimes when she talks about her frustration, that is all I see about her. She is not my wife who has strengths and qualities that I admire. She is the person who is discontent being a homemaker.

Pastor: That is a very helpful insight, Bill. The anger you are experiencing keeps you in a vengeful spirit and blocks you from seeing Joy's perspective and even seeing her as a complete person.

Joy: It feels that way too. When Bill gets angry about this issue, I feel like I am Joy the discontented mom, rather than Joy that has all sorts of things going on in her life, including struggling with being at home.

Pastor: It is important to remember that understanding and agreement are not necessarily the same thing. To see things from another person's perspective does not mean that you have to see their viewpoint as valid. Bill, you may not like Joy's perspective, but it will help your anger with her if you seek to understand why she has that perspective.

This interaction is a beautiful blend of teaching, counseling, and marital understanding. The pastor could have laid out the three issues from Augsburger's book and moved on to the next topic. What he has done is talked about the first point by describing it in summary form. In this role, he is playing more of a teaching or educative function. He is not quoting the book directly but paraphrasing the salient issues. Then there is an opportunity for Bill to interact with the material and process it. In the current situation, Bill has understood and has processed it well. The pastor reinforces this by commending Bill, and then Joy is able to give her perspective. In contrast to sermons, where teaching is usually one way and the speaker does not have the opportunity to understand how the congregation is processing what is being said, the counseling environment allows for clarification on all sides.

Pastor: The second component of forgiveness is valuing others. A logical extension of seeking to understand others is an ability to value and respect them. As people created in the image of God, and in our case redeemed by Jesus Christ, we are those that need to offer each other the gift of value. In this sense, no one is unlovable or undeserving of our forgiveness and compassion. Bill, for you to forgive Joy and not react in anger will require that you see her as someone that is valuable.

Bill: That is not a hard concept to understand and it is one that I believe, but it is easy to forget when you are in the heat of the moment.

Pastor: This brings us to Augsburger's third point, one that ties nicely into our discussion on Romans 12. He suggests that the third component of forgiveness is loving the other person. This quality is not something we can manufacture, but is something that is a gift from God. It is the divine power that allows us to feed our enemy when he is hungry or give her drink when she is thirsty. As we serve, help, give, and minister to others we become continually strengthened to complete the work of forgiveness in the sense that we are not holding things against others.

We believe it is important for pastors to have thought through the dynamics of forgiveness if they are going to help people who are struggling with anger. In the current situation, Bill and Joy are struggling with issues that are difficult, but not debilitating. However, pastors will be called on to deal with people who have experienced horrific abuse in the context of the family or the church. The anger in these situations is intense and it is easy to trivialize it by pushing people into instant forgiveness. We need to recognize the complexity in forgiveness and the need to work people through it with discernment and sensitivity. A husband and wife team, Sidney and Suzanne Simon (1990), have written about the intricacy of forgiveness by suggesting that forgiveness needs to be characterized by nine qualities.

1. Forgiveness is a by-product of an ongoing healing process.
2. Forgiveness is an internal process.

3. Forgiveness is a sign of positive self-esteem.
4. Forgiveness is letting go of the intense emotions attached to incidents from our past.
5. Forgiveness is recognizing that we no longer need our grudges and resentments, our hatred and self-pity.
6. Forgiveness is no longer wanting to punish the people who hurt us.
7. Forgiveness is accepting that nothing we do to punish them will heal us.
8. Forgiveness is freeing up and putting to better use the energy once consumed by holding grudges, harboring resentments, and nursing unhealed wounds.
9. Forgiveness is moving on.

Joy: Talking about this has brought more understanding to the passage you had us read in Luke 17. Forgiveness seems to be something that we are responsible to give others, quite apart from what they have done to us. I had always thought that you could only forgive someone if they repented genuinely. In the Luke 17 passage, the same person comes back after sinning seven times in one day and says, I repent. There is no way that the person could have been genuine. Otherwise, they would not have kept sinning. But Jesus still says we are to forgive.

Bill: It's no wonder the disciples asked the Lord to increase their faith. You would need a lot of faith to live that way.

Pastor: Do you remember Jesus' response to their demand, Bill?

Bill: Yeah, he started talking about faith as a mustard seed and how you do not need much faith. Then he tells this parable which sounds a little harsh to me.

Pastor: In what way?

Bill: Well, there's this servant who has worked all day. He has to come home and feed his master first and the master does not even thank him. Jesus says that this was the right way because that is what servants are supposed to do. They are unworthy people doing their duty.

Pastor: Why do you think Jesus told this parable?

Bill: Even though it sounds harsh, I think he was emphasizing that forgiving is our responsibility. It is something we are supposed to do and it is not much influenced by how others respond to us. It almost seems that forgiveness is a one-way street. We are responsible to forgive, whatever is done to us and however the person responds after.

Joy: But I still don't get the "forgive and forget" line. I hear that all the time. I think of Bill and some of the things that happened to him in his home. I believe he has an attitude of forgiveness, but he still remembers. Is that wrong?

Pastor: Do you remember the verse in Jeremiah 31:34 where God says that he will forgive our wickedness and will remember our sins no more? What do you think "remember" means in that verse?

Bill: That reminds me. I just heard someone in the church quote that verse about forgetting the past. Does that tie in?

Pastor: You are referring to Philippians 2:13 where Paul talks about forgetting what is behind. Let's put these two verses together. First of all, we need to note that God is eternal and infinite. He does not forget like we do. His capacities are such that nothing escapes his mind or his memory. So when he talks about not remembering our sins, he is not referring to memory. Obviously, God knows what we have done and where we have fallen short. Whether it was yesterday, last week, or last year, it is not out of his memory. But when we are Christians he does not hold our sin against us. It is not over our head or staring us in the face. His forgiveness keeps our slate clean.

Joy: That is helpful to understand because I have found the "forgive and forget" line hard to understand. If we have a brain and a memory, I would think that past events would still be retained. But what about the Philippians 2 passage?

Pastor: It is interesting to note that early in the same chapter Paul talks about his background, how he was circumcised, of the people of Israel, of the tribe of Benjamin, a Hebrew, and a Pharisee, along with a number of other historical facts. Then he talks about taking all these historical issues and weighing them up against the knowledge of Christ. In fact, he uses the image of profit and loss to discuss this. His history comes out as loss and Christ comes out as profit. In that context, he says that he is forgetting the past. Again, he is not wiping his past from his memory. In fact, if he had obliterated it from memory he would not have been able to talk about it early in the chapter. He is not counting it as crucial. It is not running his life. He is not going to rely on his past successes.

Passive, Aggressive, and Assertive Responses

If anger and vengeance are the antidote to love and forgiveness, then we need to ask about how this relationship shows up when it comes to the marital interaction. We might expect that Bill and Joy will have a different quality of communication when they are in the anger-vengeance mode than the love-forgiveness framework. Apart from the Christian aspects to these issues, the pastor needs to explore how these work out in the marital communication.

Pastor: I would like to shift the focus a little and talk about your marital communication as it ties in to what we have been talking about tonight. The issues of vengeance and forgiveness have an effect on our communication styles and I would like to discuss that for a little while. Essentially, there are three different options—passive, aggressive, and assertive.

The passive or nonassertive approach to communication focuses on seeking to please others by yielding, placating, or giving in. People who adopt this approach to relationships will tend to implode their anger because they do not want to run the risk of losing the relationship. This would result in the blocking of their needs to be accepted, appreciated, and affirmed. They might tend to bury their vengeance and to inaccurately think they have forgiven the other person even though the anger is still raging inside.

The aggressive approach to communication looks exactly the opposite. The emphasis is on getting your own way and making demands on others. People who adopt this approach will tend to explode with their anger and become quite over-bearing toward others. They tend not to respect others or value them and their major relational style is control and dominance. Often they will have others who will get along with them, but only because the aggressive person has exerted his/her power.

It is not uncommon for people to fluctuate between passivity and aggressiveness. I remember dealing with an associate pastor a number of years ago who would let things accumulate over time and appeared to be quite tolerant. Then, all of a sudden, or so it seemed, he would lash out at people and become quite overbearing. In the community, he created an atmosphere of unpredictability because people were not sure which side they were going to see. At one moment his anger seemed under control, and at the next it was raging.

The third style is the assertive one. In a sense, this is a compromise position between the two extremes. The emphasis is on respect for one's own values and convictions, along with those held by others. Power is shared so that one person or opinion does not dominate or become subservient. When assertive people become angry they do not lash out and blame others. Nor do they internalize what they are feeling and never bring it out into the open. They are willing to experience the risk in community by sharing what they are going through with integrity.

Bill: I have heard a little about these three styles in the past, but it sure helps to give you a perspective on the way people respond in church. I have often sensed that some people are angry, but are not dealing with it directly and openly. Other people seem so intent on getting their own way that they bully and threaten through their anger. It seems to me that the assertive style is the most oriented to community building. Not only are you being yourself and expressing yourself freely, you are also validating other people's ability to be themselves.

Pastor: That is so true, Bill. In fact, I am concerned that all three of these styles could be linked with the individual and their rights and their needs. What we need to do, it seems to me, is look at these styles to see how they nurture and build community. Any thoughts on that, Joy?

Joy: Passivity and aggressiveness seem to wipe other people out. In passivity you are wiping yourself out, and with aggressiveness you are denying everyone else. Neither of these seems to allow for the full development of community.

Bill: You know, I am embarrassed to admit this, but I was just linking all of this with our marital tension. I think I am one of those people you described as flipping from passivity to aggressiveness. When I do that, I am either negating my own values or ignoring Joy's.

Pastor: That is an important insight, Bill. I wonder if this ties in with some of the family of origin material we looked at in one of our earlier sessions. The little child in you finds it easier to feel inadequate and put down, so the passive response makes sense. But then it accumulates and it is easy to let it fly.

Joy: I think a similar but different thing happens to me. Because there was no occasion for anger in my family, it was never necessary for me to get aggressive. There was no one to compete with. Passivity was the best option. You would make everyone happy, make sure they stayed happy, and feel confident that your yielding and placating would make them accept you. Coming into marriage I have had to readjust. When Bill lets his anger out aggressively, I am becoming more aware of my own anger and can sometimes let him have it. Parenting, in fact, has really brought this to the surface. Sometimes the kids push my buttons for so long that I lose it. But because I am in unfamiliar territory, I do not know how to respond.

Pastor: Let me give you a couple of simple concepts to keep in mind in this area. Just knowing the information is not going to change your style, but it might give you a greater understanding of what is happening, both inside of you and in each other. The concepts revolve around three words: freedom, worth, and community. In a healthy relationship there is a permission for freedom. Each person is free to experience and express their experiences. There is also a communication of worth. When freedom is exercised, both the person who is expressing their experience and the person who is the recipient communicate a sense of value and worth, both of themselves and each other. Finally, there is an affirmation of community. Both parties act and react in a way that facilitates the relationship so that neither person is negated or disaffirmed.

Bill: It sounds to me like remembering those concepts could keep us on track when we are confused by our anger.

Homework

Pastor: I am encouraged by a lot of what has gone on in our session tonight. As you know, next week is our fifth session so I would like to suggest you do some reflecting between now and next week. I would like you to summarize the key things you have learned in our sessions together, the significant changes that you have been able to implement, and the areas that you think you need to work on. I would like you to focus on this exercise individually, rather than as a couple.

7

ALIENATION AND RECONCILIATION
SESSION 5

Summary: The final session concludes with two themes that are important in the disengagement stage: referral and termination. Principles for dealing with referral are examined along with salient issues that need to be considered in termination. The pastor walks Bill and Joy through a recapturing of the key concerns in the counseling. The chapter ends with a brief comment on the power of anger to alienate or reconcile.

Possibility of Referral

One of the concerns that pastors must deal with in strategic counseling is whether they should refer. Since the time parameters have been set, the pastor needs to be thinking about referral before the fifth session and the rationale needs to be clear. Seven questions need to be answered in order to determine the why and the how of referral.

Why are you referring?

Under normal circumstances, referrals take place when the pastor is beyond his/her level of competence, a different style of help is required, the pastor cannot provide the time that is needed, or there are dynamics between the pastor and parishioner that are counterproductive. These might include sexual involvement, excessive dependence, or irresolvable conflict. The psychoanalytic school of therapy has taught us a lot about the power of countertransference, where the counselor begins to have his/her personal needs met through a misconstrual of the roles in counseling. So pastors who believe that they are falling in love with a parishioner after two sessions of counseling may not fully understand their personal historical dynamics that may have led to such an erroneous conclusion.

Pastors need to keep in mind that the assessment of competence is a process that all counselors need to practice. Good counselors are not those who believe they can help everyone. In fact, the real distinction between experienced and inexperienced helpers is that the former group are aware of their limitations and are willing to act accordingly. Professional therapists, psychologists, psychiatrists, and the like refer regularly because they recognize that their own training and expertise limits the number of people they can help. In light of this reality, pastors need not interpret referral as a statement of inadequacy, rather, quite the opposite is true.

In Bill and Joy's case, the evaluation of the four sessions would suggest that referral is not necessary, although one might want to explore with him whether he needs to do more work on the family of origin concerns. Both Bill and Joy have made significant progress in understanding anger from a biblical perspective, have been able to process the thoughts and feelings around anger, and their behavioral anger management has improved dramatically. However, this does not imply that they will never need help again or that all their problems have been solved. Rather, they are pointing in the right direction and that may be sufficient at present.

When answering the "why?" question regarding referral and anger, keep in mind that problems often have complexity built into them. For example, Ronald and Patricia Potter-Efron (1991) have written a very helpful book that describes the link between anger management and various chemical dependencies, including alcoholism. If this link had become evident with Bill or Joy, the pastor would find it necessary to refer even if some of the anger dynamics had been addressed.

Have you dealt with your own needs to help?

One of the great ironies of helping others is that it can be self-serving. Having others contact you for help, listen to your direction, and appreciate your input can do wonders for the ego! This dynamic is particularly influential in the fifth session. Maybe the pastor has enjoyed the interaction and is grieving the loss of the person. Some pastors have their identity wrapped up in serving others and termination of counseling is quite painful. There are also situations where pastors have an inaccurate view of their own competence, and struggle with referral because they see themselves as the only one who can provide the help that is needed. From a Christian perspective, an understanding that God uses all of us to minister, at different times and at different places, will greatly alleviate the pressure to do all the counseling.

Pastor Harvey needs to look inside as he approaches the last session and ask himself if he is willing to refer if that is necessary. Is he able to move Bill and Joy into another helping venue if he is beyond his level of competence and available time? This may seem like a simple issue, but it can be quite confusing when personal issues are strong. The desire to not refer may have more to do with the pastor's own needs than it does with competence or time.

Is the referral a surprise?

One of the most difficult things for people who have been referred is that it has taken them by surprise. They are not expecting it and, in fact, have interpreted the referral as an act of rejection on the part of the pastor. The best way to avoid this problem is to let them know right at the beginning that you want to help them in whatever way you can. (i.e. "I am very happy to be of help to you. We may find that what I can offer you is not enough. If that happens I will be happy to put you in touch with someone else.") When you do make the referral, you can refer back to this initial conversation. Keep in mind, however, that some people will still interpret the referral as being due to rejection, frustration, or your not liking them.

In short-term strategic counseling, the pastor has a natural opportunity to eliminate the surprise factor. Both the pastor and the parishioner are aware at the beginning of the process that there will be five sessions and that decisions will be made at the end of that period.

Have you made the referral clearly and specifically?

One of the reasons a lot of referrals break down is that they are made in a very general way. (i.e. "I think it would be good for you to see a counselor.") When you refer, give the name, number, and basic qualifications of the person you are referring them to see. If possible, let them know why you have selected this person and why you believe they should see this person. This requires that you know some resource people and have their names and numbers accessible. It also presupposes that you have enough knowledge of the counselor to make a specific referral.

Assume that Bill's problems with anger management have led to alcoholism. While he may have found the counseling with Pastor Harvey to be helpful, he is in need of treatment for his addiction. Do you know the counselors who have expertise in this particular problem? Have you ever met with them, received literature from them, or read anything they have written? Have you ever had them in the church to do a special seminar on addictions? Have you talked with them on the phone to find out their particular bias or orientation? Pastors who engage in this kind of data collection on local counselors are better equipped to refer clearly and specifically.

Who should you refer to?

This is a difficult question for many pastors. They are not sure who they can trust or who will provide the help that is required. A number of factors need to be kept in mind here. First of all, the research needs to be done ahead of time. Make the connections and do the networking to find out who is competent in given areas. Furthermore, always refer when there are signs of physical difficulties. Having the names of good general practitioners is valuable for a pastor who is thinking comprehensively about the problems that people face. If there are more intensive psychological difficulties that are beyond your level of experience or expertise, refer to a qualified therapist, psychologist, or psychiatrist.

Should pastors always refer to Christian professionals? Our answer to this question depends on a number of concerns. Some pastors are in areas where there are few Christian counselors so their options for referral are limited. There are Christian counselors in other areas, but they may not have competence in a given problem. It is probably wise to start with recognized expertise as the primary concern. If there is a Christian that has this expertise, then they would be the prime candidate. They would have an understanding and a sensitivity to the spiritual dimensions of the problem, along with an ability to cope with the particular difficulty.

We do need to recognize the diversity in the Christian counseling world. For example, in areas like divorce, remarriage, homosexuality, and sexuality in general, the viewpoints among Christian counselors vary dramatically. If Bill and Joy's problems with anger were moving them toward divorce, the pastor would need to be aware that referral to a Christian marriage counselor does not guarantee the permanence of the marriage. Pastors need to exercise discernment in this area, keeping in mind the needs of the parishioner, their own personal convictions, and the theological position of the church.

How does the referral take place?

Often the pastor will phone the counselor in order to determine basic information and their availability. Counselors will respond in various ways to this kind of call, but it is usually best to keep the conversation brief and focus on the basics of the counseling situation. The counselor does not want to know your interpretation and understanding of the case, but the essential details of what is happening. Too much information at this time will lead the counselor to become less objective, and also put him/her in the uncomfortable position of knowing information that the counselee may not wish to share. A sample conversation follows:

> Dr. Stone, it's Pastor Harvey. I don't know if you remember me but we chatted briefly when you spoke at the last ministerial. I wanted to check on your availability to see if you could speak with a couple I have been seeing for the past month or so.
>
> Yes, I do remember you. Thanks for calling. I do have an opening coming up on Tuesday nights from 8:00–9:00. Do you think this couple could come at that time?
>
> Actually, that would probably work out well for them. But I would have to check to be absolutely sure.
>
> Can you tell me a little bit about the difficulties they are having and why you are referring them to me?
>
> I have met with them three times and they are struggling with anger management. But in the last session Bill, the husband, indicated that he was drinking pretty heavily as a way of managing his anger. As we explored it, I found that this is a long-standing problem that is beyond my level of training. When you talked at the ministerial about ways you work with addictive people I thought you would be a good person to meet with him.
>
> That's helpful. Why don't you have them call me so we can set up the time? Tell me Bill's full name so I will know who it is when he calls.

The pastor has provided Dr. Stone with enough information to explain the referral and the general nature of the problem. From here, it is usually best to allow the parishioner to make the contact and make the call themselves. If the pastor sets up the appointment or convinces the counselor to phone the parishioner, an unhealthy precedent is set up and it makes it difficult to determine whether the person needing help was genuinely desirous of it. If the parishioner is "chased" he/she may lean on the helpers in all aspects of the helping and not take appropriate responsibility for his/her own healing.

How do you respond after a referral?

When you refer, stay out of the process as much as possible. It is wise to check to see that the contact has been made. It is also appropriate to reassure the parishioner after they have been going to the counselor for a while (i.e. "I am praying for you"), but resist the temptation to fish for details. Most of us will find ourselves naturally making comparisons between our style and the counselor's. This tendency will be fed when the person comes back and says, "I liked you better." However, it is crucial that we communicate to the person that we are still committed to the referral as it was made originally. It is easy to "take someone back" after we have "let them go." In this area we also need to remember that counseling is not always enjoyable. A person's complaint that they are not "enjoying" the counseling may be a sign of resistance to growth, not a reflection of poor counseling.

In our experience, it is extremely helpful if pastors and counselors can work together in the healing process (Wilson, 1995). This approach requires a level of trust between the two helpers and a willingness to admit that both individual and professional counseling can dovetail with spiritual and communal interventions from the church. When the pastor and the counselor are committed to this approach to help, they need to discuss the parameters around what information will be shared and why. They also need to communicate with the parishioner and be sensitive to their needs and preferences. In this case, the pastor remains part of the healing process even after the referral has been made.

The Disengagement Stage

Since this is intended to be the last session, there are a number of very important objectives to bear in mind. Also, considering that it has been a few weeks since the last session, there may be much to deal with that has come out of their relationship during that time. First, let's think about this consideration. When there has been a long gap between sessions, the pastor must carefully bring himself up to date by reviewing notes and carefully planning the strategy that will bring the counseling to an appropriate conclusion. Personal preparation for this session will be very important. Remaining issues need to be dealt with. Loose ends need to be tied up. Bill and Joy need to be left with a clear sense of their responsibility to continue working on their issues. They need to leave with a sense of accomplishment, hope, and motivation for the future. If it is appropriate and necessary, issues of referral or a clear sense of how to deal with any unresolvable issues that may arise in the future need to be in place. One can readily see that much hinges upon this session.

This session is the disengagement stage of the counseling process. An affirmation of the pastoral counselor-parishioner role would be appropriate, along with a reminder that we now transition to the pastor-parishioner role with an acknowledgment that the partnership in each case may be somewhat different. Affirming the continued relationship in the pastor's role is important. Second, it is frequently important in this session to review again questions of confidentiality and to deal with any fears that their issues will be used illustratively or in any other way by the pastor. Sometimes it is important to discourage reading into things the pastor may say as being a reference to their situation. Sometimes a touch of paranoia may lead people to assume oblique references are being made to them when this is not the case, but a more general reference to the struggles we all deal with. Third, it is good to assure them of the continuing ministry of the Holy Spirit in their lives as they continue to seek spiritual maturity and fulfillment of their gifts in ministry. This is important, inasmuch as some Christians feel that when they acknowledge struggles church leadership may deem them unsuitable for ministry within the church. An acknowledgment of struggles in our spiritual journey needs to be accompanied by the affirmation that struggles do not disqualify from ministry.

The disengagement stage should involve a reflection upon the counseling experience wherein honesty and vulnerability to consider tensions, deficiencies, or times when clarity was lacking may be acknowledged. If one wishes to encourage others to acknowledge shortcomings in functioning so that they may be dealt with, it is important that pastors and counselors acknowledge falling short as well. It might be very helpful for a pastoral counselor to acknowledge that in the last session, upon reflection, he realized he missed the point of what was being communicated. Let's not impose on ourselves perfectionism or assumptions that grow out of pride any more than we would on others. The demonstration of honesty and openness in this process of reflection may be very instructive to Bill and Joy.

An important part of the disengagement stage will be the review and summary of what has been dealt with, what has been learned, what has been implemented, and the benefits derived from this. The pastor is not seeking here to receive some backslapping but to affirm learning, the assumption of responsibility for implementation, an opportunity to encourage continuance by identifying successes achieved, and to encourage Bill and Joy to acknowledge and affirm the changes they have witnessed in each other. The latter is important. It is true that the removal of incidents of negative input (invalidation) to each other enhances the relationship more quickly than positive input. However, teaching couples the benefit and art of affirming one another is also important. Paul, in the Acts of the Apostles, uses a number of concepts to express this role. In Acts 13:43 and 14:22 he speaks of exhorting or persuading believers to continue in the faith or the grace of God. This is an appropriate role for the pastoral counselor. As he revisited churches, Paul established his attempt to "strengthen the brethren" in a variety of ways (Acts 15:41; 16:5; 18:23). One of the New Testament words that excites us is the word for comfort, which basically means to be called alongside another. In the Old Testament when Noah was born his father said, "He will comfort us . . ." (Gen. 5:29). This word came to be used in a variety of ways, such as Ruth 1:9 when Naomi said to her daughters-in-law, "May the LORD grant that each of you will find rest." It is used many times in relation to God's care and comfort of people or of people in relation to each other. The Hebrew word means "to cause to breathe again, to relieve or to provide a resting place." In marriage counseling, it is important to encourage spouses to develop the art of causing each other to breathe again through the art of comforting one another.

In the New Testament, the word "comfort" is often translated by the word "encouragement." It is crucial to assist spouses to learn this ministry to each other, and the counseling environment is often an excellent place to begin to learn this art. Of course, another New Testament definition of our ministry to one another is expressed in the word "edification," which means to build up the other. It is appropriate to express the spousal relationship in this biblical imagery. Couples will often be strengthened in their relationship as we help them to define that relationship in biblical images or concepts. The spousal relationship may best be described as a relationship of grace where each responds to the other out of love, enabled by the Spirit rather than simply as obligation growing out of our covenant. Obligation is part of covenant, but pleasure in the relationship of covenant is an outgrowth of grace. Grace is an expression of love offered freely and unconditionally by the lover, rather than a response to what is deserved. It is very important to underline the question of commitment in marriage, which is often expressed by the term "covenant." This is a rich term, receiving its richness through God's use of it to describe his commitment to his people in the Old Testament. However, there is a pitfall here. Quite frequently believers will emphasize the obligation or binding dimension of covenant and such an emphasis can convert covenant into a legal bondage. An alert pastor will pick up the nuances in the relationship, communication, imagery used, or physical posturing by the couple that will indicate a relationship based upon obligation.

We need to emphasize and experience the grace, worship, and pleasure dimensions of the covenant relationship. The covenant is initiated by God's love and his overwhelming grace in giving himself to such a relationship of exclusivity to his chosen people. His desire is intimacy, the joy of reciprocal generosity, which leads to worship and the pleasure of belonging in the security of mutual commitment. In our culture, marriage is a contract which, at its best, is entered for the mutual benefit of each. Without the component of grace and joyful generosity, it may become an economic contract designed to fulfill pleasure defined as self-fulfillment or self-actualization. Along with the security that comes from the freely-entered-into obligation of covenant, we desire to lead couples to the graceful expression of generosity which issues in joy for both giver and receiver. Such is the pathway to intimacy. The power of obligation which issues in security is swallowed up in grace resulting in joyful security. The door to intimacy swings wide open in the presence of the vulnerability made possible by that joyful security.

Additionally, in this session it is important to clearly identify remaining work to be done in the relationship. The experience of growth is not finished yet. It is helpful to leave the couple with a sense of progress, along with the continuing need to seek growth in effective communicating and relating. The establishment of goals and plans for the future should be clearly outlined. In fact, we would recommend the writing out of such intentions and the achievement of a clear commitment to work at these. Building in some accountability through a commitment for feedback at some future date may strengthen their resolve. This anticipation of future areas of difficulty or adjustment may provide an expectation that will inhibit the sense of surprise that might provide a considerable stumbling block at some future time. It is far more helpful to be realistic about future issues than to create a false expectation that everything will be rosy from here on.

Principles for Termination

The following verses describe a very important principle in relationships:

> For this reason a man will leave his father and mother and be united to his wife, and they will become one flesh. (Gen. 2:24)

If anyone comes to me and does not hate his father and mother, his wife and children, his brothers and sisters—yes, even his own life— he cannot be my disciple. (Luke 14:26)

In summary, you need to leave before you cleave. You need to move out of one sphere well before you move into another one. This can be applied in terms of marriage or our relationship with the Lord, as well as relationships in general. In counseling, this process of leaving is described as termination.

In essence, termination is another commencement. It is a direct way of indicating that the parishioner can function on their own without the pastor. If you understand termination in this way, it will help you understand the feelings people have at termination. What did Bill and Joy experience at the beginning of these five sessions? fear? ambivalence? wondering if it is worth it? These questions take place at the end of counseling as well. In fact, as Bill and Joy come into the office they start off with these kinds of issues.

> *Bill:* I feel odd that we are at the end of our five sessions. At times I have struggled to come to see you, but now that it is over it is like I am on my own. Part of this feels good because I believe progress has been made, but it is also a little scary.
>
> *Joy:* I'm with Bill on this one! These sessions have become pretty central in my life. I have looked forward to them each week and found that the homework gave me focus and direction. I worry that I may slip back into old patterns.
>
> *Pastor:* I appreciate your sharing these feelings. Your responses are normal and natural. When you have worked hard and focused on resolving some difficulties, it brings energy and enthusiasm. To think that it may end is not easy. Let's talk about some of the issues involved in terminating our counseling relationship and try to recapture some of what we have learned together.

Termination feelings usually give evidence as to the real goals of counseling. This is true for both the pastor and the parishioner.

Some of us, as pastors, feel inadequate and useless when the counseling is over. In responding this way we are implicitly revealing some of our goals. If the pastor is counseling to meet needs for affection, approval, or dependence, then termination will be greeted with pain. In fact, in these situations pastors may postpone termination so these needs continue to be met. The same thing may happen if the pastor wants all the parishioners to feel good in counseling. With some people that goal may never be realized so the counseling will never stop.

If a parishioner wants to be reliant and dependent on someone, termination is going to raise a lot of uncertainty and fear. Similarly, if they are in counseling because it is one of the few solid relationships they have, termination will bring feelings of abandonment and rejection.

In short-term strategic counseling, the goals need to be clear at the beginning so that the ending can bring closure. The goals may vary depending on the situation:

difficulties are realistically perceived

new insight and strength has been achieved

difficulties are integrated into whole being

problems are being discussed much easier

new relationships have been developed

new problem-solving styles have been learned

new information and facts have been absorbed

In the current situation, the pastor has acknowledged the feelings expressed by Bill and Joy and has expressed a willingness to discuss termination concerns. At least three issues need to be addressed.

1. All parties need to be aware that the termination of the counseling relationship is taking place. Pastors and parishioners have other roles that they play in their relationships with each other. It may be in a home study fellowship or an adult Sunday school class. It may be socializing at the church picnic or working on the building committee together. In Strategic Pastoral Counseling, they have had a particular and defined role, namely, counselor and counselee. At the end of five sessions this is over, a reality that needs to be accepted by all parties.

In general, there are three types of termination. The first is a natural outcome of the fact that the agreed upon goals for counseling have been met. In Strategic Pastoral Counseling, the goals are somewhat time related (i.e. five sessions), but they may also be growth related (i.e. when the communication is more open with your wife). In the second type of termination, the counseling ceases because the parishioner does not return. Various reasons may be given for this response, including finances, travel time, availability, frustration, pressure from others, and so on. In these situations pastors may have to deal with the lack of resolution, and, depending on their own personal history, this could create some tension. The final type of termination can be traced to external circumstances, where the pastor or the parishioner may move, go on disability, or have a prolonged illness.

2. No new material should be introduced in the last session. Termination involves that which has already taken place. Both the pastor and the parishioner are looking back and seeking to consolidate what has happened and what has been gained. It is a time of retrospection, summary, and reaction to experience. To introduce new insights or observations at this stage is to invite an extension of the agreed upon time frame. We do recognize that a traumatic incident may have arisen in the life of the parishioner just before the last session. If this occurs, the normal rule of thumb may be sacrificed, but this would be the exception rather than the rule.

There is a real sense in which the counseling process is a move from dependence to independence. Many parishioners will find it easy to depend on the pastor and the counseling process during the five sessions, but the ultimate goal is to be independent of this process and able to function on one's own. Given that termination is a new commencement, the pastor always needs to keep the future in mind.

3. There is a need to clarify the nature of future involvement. A number of questions need to be raised around this theme. Is the contact open-ended in that the parishioner can return at any point in time? Will there be future counseling contact? Who will initiate this contact? Because many relational problems come from the violation of expectations, a clarity of expectations on both sides will save unnecessary pain. In the following brief interaction, the pastor, Bill, and Joy achieve a good degree of clarity.

Pastor: This is our last session tonight, but obviously we will see each other in various contexts around the church. How do you see us connecting from this point on?

Bill: Even to this point, I have found it a little awkward to see you in the pulpit or in the adult Sunday school class. I wonder if you are thinking about us or our problems. I suppose it is a sense of shame or embarrassment.

Joy: I have not found this too hard, but I am not sure whether you will ever talk to us again about our issues with anger or whether it will be a silent subject.

Pastor: You have raised some very important issues. Let me try to respond to them. First of all, I want you to know that I will not initiate any discussion about the anger issues. If we relate around the church this subject will not come up from me. If either of you choose to give me a brief update, I have no problem with that. If the problems resurface or you sense the need of further help, give me a call and we can discuss where to go from there. We may reconnect personally or I might suggest another avenue for help, but I would definitely be open to helping you plot the direction.

Summarizing and Reflecting

Pastor: It has been a few weeks since we met and I expect you have some important things to share. Let me suggest some direction for this session since it will be our last, at least for now. We want to review the time we have had together, to identify the key learning that you have acquired and the changes you have achieved (which was part of the homework you were going to do for today), but we would also benefit from reflecting on the counseling experience. Reflecting on the counseling experience may be understood as reviewing the journey we have taken together. Should we have traveled faster or slower at certain points? Should we have stopped to view more scenery along the way? What was most helpful? What was most difficult or unclear? Did we begin with similar expectations or respond to each other's expectations? Did we achieve the goals we set or did we change them along the way? Another question we need to ask ourselves is: Where do we go from here? Are there specific areas we can identify that we particularly need to seek understanding or change in? It is my hope that by looking at some of these questions we can further our learning and consolidate what we have achieved. One of the things we asked you to do over these past few weeks was to summarize or select a few of the things we have shared in our sessions that you have learned, found helpful, or implemented. Could you briefly share that with me now?

Joy: I see a change in the way we relate. I think it is an improvement from one perspective in that we are talking more and not withdrawing. On the other hand, I am uncomfortable because we express anger more freely and I don't always know how to deal with that. Coming to understand my frustration as anger and an inappropriate or ineffective way to express my anger was helpful, but, again, I am not sure I like to see myself as an angry person. Last time it became evident that my lack of fulfillment at home and lack of freedom to develop professionally was a big part of my anger, especially when I did not experience understanding of that from Bill. You talked about vengeance growing out of anger. It was hard for me to acknowledge those feelings. Forgiveness feels good to me as an idea, but I'm not sure I really know how to practice it.

Pastor: At this point, Joy, let me just suggest, in response to what you have said, that your discomfort in more overtly expressing anger is understandable, considering that most of us have some discomfort with anger, and, as you indicated earlier, you didn't have a model for the expression of anger in your home when growing up. However, overt expression is part of acknowledging and accepting anger. It is better to do that than to bury it and get into the confusion of neither of you knowing what's going on in your experience. From that point of view, the more frequent expression of anger is positive, a form of communication. Anger provides a pathway to self-exploration and self-understanding. When we communicate effectively, we may expand self-understanding to mutual understanding. The how of expression becomes the important issue. Realizing in our lives the dynamic of forgiveness is something we need to discuss and understand more fully. Bill, perhaps you could share with us your thoughts.

The pastor at this point seeks to reinforce the idea of anger expression being positive, although disconcerting, to someone unaccustomed to acknowledging and accepting it. He chooses not to respond to Joy's summary, in case such a response would influence inappropriately what Bill presents as his summary.

> *Bill:* Well, Joy made reference to more expression of anger. I disagree—
> *Pastor:* Excuse me, Bill. It would be more helpful for you to express your summary of personal learning than to focus on Joy's statement.

This response may be difficult for pastors because of the confrontational nature of this response. However, it is important for the pastor to orchestrate the session in a way that is going to be helpful, and at this point it may be quite distracting to introduce a conflictual situation. The principle of encouraging counselees to own their own feelings or responses and to express themselves, rather than correcting or critiquing the other person, is essential to effective communication. It may be useful to come back to this issue later in the session but, at the moment, it is necessary to keep Bill on track rather than permitting diversion.

> *Bill:* OK. Let me see, I made some notes. Learning that my anger was in some way anchored in my childhood and that

my response was triggered in the present helps me to see that I need to understand the present in a different way. I think for me a breach of my self-worth, which I experience when I feel rejected or criticized, activates my anger. This whole idea of the base for my self-acceptance and how dependent I am on Joy, as became clear in our last session, for certain things to reinforce my worth was hard for me to accept. Seeing the importance of acknowledging and accepting anger as often representing values and expectations which should be affirmed was important because it means my anger is not always sin. These are some of the important things I've learned.

Pastor: Thanks, Bill. It is interesting to me that each of you have focused and expressed yourselves in somewhat different ways. Your response, Joy, has focused more on what I would call a relational perspective. That is very important to you. Relationships of warmth and interaction have been important to you. Whereas, Bill, your tendency has been to focus more on a cognitive understanding of the subject. You have a strong desire to understand, to make sense, to thoughtfully process what you are giving attention to. You may be interested to know that this is quite typical as a difference between men and women. Now, if we can honor that difference we can benefit by seeing the different perspectives as complimentary, rather than competitive. Before we continue with our review, I feel I need to inquire as to whether you, Bill, feel the need to go back to the point at which I interrupted you.

Bill: Maybe I don't need to go back to that. Let me just say I was disappointed that Joy focused on "more expression of anger" when I felt we had done better than that and the reference to my not understanding kind of rubbed me the wrong way. Yet, now I've kind of lost my steam about that. I don't feel the same energy or need to respond to that.

Pastor: It is not so important for you to challenge her now. Do you understand why?

Bill: I think in processing it a bit more, I realize that "more anger" was not a criticism and the reference to my not understanding her needs was more a reference to the past. You know the session we had last time about my dependence upon Joy and her need for professional and social fulfillment was really hard for me to get around.

Pastor: Two things, Bill. Processing Joy's comment led to a different understanding. Your initial autopilot response was defensive, subjective, growing out of your sense of inadequacy, rather than a response to what Joy said. Is that a fair comment?

Bill: Yeah, I think that is right.

Pastor: So, a pause to shift from autopilot to a position of listening with acceptance and humility may be an important practice for you to implement.

Bill: So, I should count to ten or, maybe, twenty.

Pastor: Well, that's one possibility. Another possibility would be to preplan through anticipation how you will respond. One of the best ways to change behavior is to anticipate a future experience, identify the knee-jerk response, and plan a different, more effective response that we will purposefully activate when the situation arises. Intentionally, force yourself to listen to the other person rather than to your own inner world of anxiety. This is a shift in focus. This interchange illustrates the reality that often our anger comes from our own anxiety, rather from the person providing the trigger to releasing that anxiety or fear.

Bill: I'm going to work on that one.

Pastor: I believe you'll achieve that goal. I mentioned there were two things. The other was your reference to how hard it was for you to accept Joy's need for professional and social fulfillment. I knew this was hard for you in our last session and I think it is helpful to come back to it. The discussion we had last time around understanding the other person's perspective, rather than responding with vengeance, was heavy going.

Bill: You can say that again. I've thought a lot about that. I'm not sure I can express it well, but I wonder about what Joy's needs for social and professional fulfillment was triggering in me. I asked myself if I wanted her to be dependent on me to meet her social needs or dependent upon me for our financial needs. I don't know what to think about that.

Pastor: One way to get some insight on those hard questions is to ask yourself where you have seen that dependency present or what you would personally gain if it were the case for you.

Bill: You know what? The financial dependency thing was certainly evident in my family. My father took great pride in being the sole provider for his family. He worked hard and long to do that and my mother accepted it. Maybe that's the model I'm trying to follow. If that's the case, then Joy's working or her financial success would mean I wasn't the sole provider.

Pastor: Could that be further fueled by a sense of failure or inadequacy if you are not the sole provider?

Bill: I guess it could. Maybe that goes back to my being the kid who can't.

Joy: But, Bill, you have more than adequately provided. I don't see my desire to work or to be professionally successful as making any comment about you. You've done exceptionally well at work. I never thought about it having anything to do with "providing." There, again, in my family I never gave a thought about issues of who provided what and, for that reason, don't even think about that. I didn't know that was an issue in your family.

Bill: Well, it wasn't so much that it was an issue as that it just was and, I guess, I just picked up the idea and made it another issue related to my insecurity.

Joy: Well, let's not let that be an issue for us. I admire you for your provision. We can just pool our resources.

Bill: Thanks for that assurance.

Pastor: Your mutual support and affirmation of each other can be a great source of strength. Bill, let me pursue the other part of that question. Could there be some of your need present in your response to Joy's desire for social fulfillment outside the home?

Bill: Oh, I expect so. I'm probably quite jealous of Joy. I guess I'm afraid to compete with others for her attention. I can hardly believe I'm spilling my guts like this, but I'm afraid if she gets involved with too many others, I'll look bad by comparison.

Joy: Oh, Bill, that would never happen.

Pastor: Bill, I have to tell you that you look good when you spill your guts. Your tenderness and emotionality come through when you are vulnerable. When you shift from your competent, cognitive, thinking self and share your more vulnerable, feeling self, you look good. But that is not easy. It is very important that each of you provides a safe environment in which you can each be vulnerable and share your fears and concerns. Only in such honesty is there a possibility that each of you can be what the other needs you to be. Bill, you may benefit greatly from getting to know this "little boy" in you, the kid that can't. And you need to get to know the man who can. Maybe the little boy is a phantom that you need to leave behind and come to see yourself as the strong and capable person you have shown yourself to be in adulthood.

The pastor made the decision to go back to Bill's desire to focus on his disagreement with Joy. The ensuing interaction was extremely important, even though the original intention of proceeding with a summary was set aside. When growth appears to be occurring, it is important to go with it. Bill and Joy are evidencing in this interaction the potential they have acquired to deal with each other in a more mature way. Bill is discovering that being vulnerable is not life threatening, and in disclosing his fears he may experience a resolution of those fears. This interchange focuses the anger clearly in the person experiencing it, but also acknowledges the stimulus that the other person provides. One must raise the possibility that the freedom that Bill has shown may have been facilitated by the context of the counseling relationship. It is important to encourage the transition of this style of honest communication to the relationship at home.

Pastor: Without taking anything away from what you have experienced in the past few minutes, I would like us to understand more fully what has transpired. Let me ask you to try to get in touch with what you were each feeling and thinking.

Joy: I had no idea what was behind Bill's response to me about either the question of my professional needs or my social needs. When I hear that, I feel very compassionate and want to draw close to him.

Bill: Well, I felt scared in being vulnerable. But when Joy expresses understanding, I feel accepted or, I don't know if it's the right word or not, exonerated. I feel loved and I like that.

Pastor: Let me remind you of what we talked about in our last session. You remember me mentioning Augsburger's three points about forgiveness: understanding the other, valuing the other, and loving the other person. When you feel understood, valued, and loved, you are free, exonerated. That kind of forgiveness moves us from alienation to reconciliation and that feels good. The process is to respond with humility in honoring the other's perspective through exploring it to the point of achieving understanding. That may involve understanding the origin of another's fears or anxieties and understanding how the other's values, expectations, or self-worth was breached. We must deal with each other gently as we get behind each other's masks. This requires setting aside pride and vengeance to discover forgiveness, which, in turn, leads to the conversion of alienation into reconciliation. These broad biblical concepts may inhibit learning if we don't tie our concrete behavior to them. Cognitive understanding must be converted into concrete behavior. When anger expresses itself in exasperation or uncontrolled emotion, it often is an expression of sin. We may express anger as a prideful action, attack others in vengeance, or withdraw in alienation. The seeking of change for these behaviors will more frequently occur if we have an accepting environment where we can understand what is driving us from within and/or what is provoking us from without. The two of you have demonstrated in our time together today that there is a synergistic relationship between vulnerability as expressed by one person and the response of compassion on the part of the other.

The pastor is attempting to summarize and draw together an understanding of the process of change by using the experience of Bill and Joy as an immediate illustration. With Christian people, who begin with Bill's original question as to the relevance of biblical faith to the personal issue of anger, it is important to make this abundantly clear and to express it in theological language rather than the language of behavioral psychology. However, it is also important to be behavior specific to avoid the spiritualizing of the issues. It is important to clarify that understanding that Bill's anger is related to the "kid who can't" in him does not free him to bruise Joy or anyone else in his expression of anger. Understanding the contributing factors to one's behavior does not free one from culpability, but it does provide the foundation of understanding which is necessary to enter the process of change.

Pastor: Could we focus for a few minutes on remembering the issues that brought you to counseling and the behaviors you wished to change?

Bill: I initiated this process because my behavioral expression of anger was not acceptable to me or to Joy, nor was I happy with the anger I felt at work. I worried that my anger was sin and inconsistent with my Christian profession. Joy and I fought too much and, to use your term, we bruised one another too much. That's what I wanted changed.

Pastor: What have you learned about your experience and expression of anger and the factors that contribute to it?

Bill: On the one hand, I now see that the experience of anger in itself may not be the key problem. The thing I need to look at is my expression of anger and what its real source is. Much of my anger is fueled by the way I feel about myself. Rather than Joy being responsible, she often just provides the trigger. I've gotten in touch with some of my own feelings about myself, but I don't think I could have done that on my own. If I feel safe and accepted, I can explore and get some understanding. You have made me feel accepted and, especially today, I felt accepted by Joy. I really hope we can learn to communicate effectively around these concerns. I feel I've made some real gains, but it is just a start. I just hope we can keep it up.

Pastor: I would affirm the progress you've made. You know, it often helps if you structure an opportunity to practice what you have learned. Make time for the two of you to get together alone when you can practice the new communication patterns. Take the pressure off to come to a decision or conclusion about something and just focus on the process of understanding each other, expressing your values and hopes, rather than focusing on issues of conflict. How would you encapsulate your learning, Joy?

Joy: Well, I've learned a lot about myself. It may not be ideal growing up without a model of conflict or without others to compete with as a child. I don't want to knock my family, but there was lots I didn't learn. I never called my frustration what it really was, so I focused on Bill's anger rather than my own. I guess I also learned to put on a mask of pleasantness and to pretend everything was alright, but inside I was boiling sometimes. Naming my anger, I think, will help me deal with it. I have to say I've learned a lot about Bill in these sessions and that's been important to me. I need to try to understand him more and respond to who he is and affirm him. I really think he is great, you know! I just get caught up sometimes in my anger about my situation and then lash out or don't try to see his perspective. I have a real sense of hope, if we can work at some of these changes in our behavior and the way we have thought about things.

Pastor: I admire both of you for the hard work you have done. It is not easy to work at some of these issues. As you seek continued spiritual growth and the ministry of the Spirit of God in your lives, the adventure of growth will continue. I want to continue to be there for you as pastor and, if it would be helpful, at some point we can get back together in the counseling office to further process things that are important to you. You will find much material in the book *Exploring Your Anger* that you have been reading to review and

renew your commitment to the understanding and principles you have learned. Let me reiterate what we discussed
earlier about confidentiality. This is important to me and I
know it is to you. I will not knowingly use anything we have
discussed in our sessions in any way publicly, nor do I think
it wise for us as we meet in other contexts of our responsibilities in the church to refer to our counseling relationship.
What we have experienced these few sessions was special
and should not impact our partnership in the ministry of the
church. You have given me the privilege of being involved
in your lives and walking with you in this adventure of
growth. I have been honored by that. Do either of you feel
you have any loose ends we need to tie up before we conclude our time together?

Bill and Joy: (in unison) No, I don't think so.

Bill: I do feel I have gained much and have a sense of direction and want to thank you for that. It has not been easy, but
it has been helpful.

Joy: I would echo that.

Pastor: Let's join hands and have a brief prayer together as
we conclude.

Alienation and Reconciliation

The topic of anger is complex and intriguing. It is a troublesome
emotion that is tied to our family history. It receives considerable
attention in Scripture, both in its link with God as well as with
humanity. It is not easy to determine when it reflects our God-
given capacity to feel emotion or when it demonstrates our essential fallenness. Fundamentally, it has the capacity to draw us closer
to each other as it exposes our goals, values, expectations, and
personal worth. But it is a double-edged sword in its ability to
alienate and distance us from others and from ourselves.

God gives us the wisdom to discern the dark and the light side
of anger.

8

FOCUSING ON
THE PASTORAL COUNSELOR

One of the major strengths of the Strategic Pastoral Counseling model is its emphasis on the counseling process being one of partnership. The pastor is not invited to play the role of expert, guru, or problem solver. Rather, the pastor is one who is a co-pilgrim, pursuing the same journey with all the ambiguity that is inherent in it. This requires a commitment to humility so that the pastoral role is not presumed to remove all the messiness from life. It also means that the pastor has an ability to truly enter into the experience of the other person. As was looked at earlier in the book, this is the core of empathy. It is the ability to sense and feel what the other person is going through and communicate that back to them so they have a sense of being deeply understood. This not only helps them clarify what they are experiencing, but it also creates a caring relational context for the counseling.

Some mistake empathy for sympathy, the latter being more of a process of identification. If you are going through something and I have experienced the same thing, then I can really relate to you. The problem with that orientation is that none of us have experienced everything so we cannot bring our own experience to every person's difficulties. In contrast, empathy makes it possible to be able to connect with anyone because my commitment is to understand what they are going through, not connect it with an identical or similar aspect in my life.

An understanding of the true nature of empathy is crucial for the pastoral counselor. However, there is a potential weakness in that understanding. We could easily say: It does not matter whether I have gone through something or not, I can still help people because I am committed to relating to them for themselves. Such a sentiment does not reflect the core of co-pilgrimage. While co-pilgrims have not understood everything about others, they do their best to become aware of various issues.

What does this mean for the topic under consideration in this book? It means that the pastor has taken the time and expended the energy to understand as much as possible about anger. Reading, reflecting, and processing will become necessary pursuits to establish clear and accurate theoretical and theological parameters. But there is also a need to struggle through the issues personally. What about your anger? How do you cope with it? Do you typically implode or explode? Is vengeance and personal animosity a struggle when you are angry? The purpose of raising these questions is not to create paranoia, but to invite the pastor to actively and personally engage with the material under consideration. This may be the greatest gift you can give to your parishioners.

Having said this, we recognize that it is difficult for many pastors to deal with their anger. With a touch of humor, David Augsburger (1979) explores the pastor and his/her anger in the context of the church.

> Ordained. It makes a difference. No anger here. (God forbid. God's people forbid.) No malicious gossip. (Although sharing a spicey prayer request may release a little ministerial tension.) No resent-

ment. (Although holding a "concern" against a sister or brother may balance a pastor's internal ledger of grievances.) No temper. (Although intense vocal expression of righteous indignation may reduce the clergy's consternation.) No irritability. (Although being a bit short in speech when feeling "burdened with the care of souls" may restore serenity.) No hostile rejection. (Although encouraging a problem maker to consider another church home may pass as peacemaking.) No wrath or rage. (Those who feel aroused simply call it by an acceptable name: righteous indignation, conviction, zeal perhaps, but never anger.) . . . As anger accumulates in the congregation's emotional system, it is the pastor who is called to defuse it, to neutralize the hostile acidity in the manner of an effervescent agape-seltzer. Pastors are supposed to be able to absorb more hostility than other professionals and to be without anger themselves. (1, 3)

To aid you in the process of struggling through your own anger issues, we would encourage you to carefully and systematically work through the questions below. They are taken from the Personal Reflection section in *Exploring Your Anger*. The degree to which you are able to both understand and articulate your own experience with anger is the degree to which you will be able to confront it in the complex world of pastoral counseling.

Chapter 1—Christians and Anger: Friends or Foes?

1. Take a closer look at community life in your church. What is the underlying message about anger? Do you have people like William, Sally, Judith, Helmut, Elisabeth, and Tom in the congregation? What impact do these different styles have on other people? How do they affect you? Do you know any of these people well enough to talk with them about their experience of anger?
2. The next time you are angry or upset, think through your experience and expression of anger as you see it by looking at our working definition. Ask yourself some questions:

a. What emotion is being displayed in the anger?

b. Can you identify the goal, value, or expectation that has been blocked?

c. Do you have a sense that your personal worth is being threatened?

If there is an absence of information in one of these areas, spend more time on it to see if you can understand your anger better. Do not focus on the effect of your anger, only your experience and expression of it.

3. List three things that really upset you at church and another three that upset you in your home environment. Rather than focusing on the trigger that precipitated your anger, zero in on your goals, values, and expectations. What are the goals, values, or expectations that are lurking behind these areas of upset? Go back in your history and see if you can link any of these with early experiences, significant events, particular people, or family themes.

4. Tell someone who knows you well that there are four major ways to express anger—suppression, repression, expression, and confession. Ask him or her which one they see you displaying the most. Talk to someone who knows you less well. Ask him or her the same question. How does this feedback mirror your own self-assessment?

5. As you function in community at your church, which orientation do you tend to fall into most regularly—personality orientation, tolerance orientation, contagious orientation, or denial orientation?

6. Reread the passages in the chapter that talk about the wrath of God. Take a concordance and look up other references to the same topic. Ask the Lord to give you fresh insight into the relationship between God's wrath and your salvation. Pray that an understanding of the depth of sin will bring a renewed appreciation for the extent of his forgiveness.

7. Jonah, Job, and the psalmist had times in their lives when they were angry with God. Have you ever experienced anger at God? What does that feel like for you? What do you do when you are angry at God?

8. Use a good concordance and/or word study book to trace some of the Old and New Testament words for anger in more depth.

9. Reflect on a recent situation where you were angry. Use the discussion of anger and sin to determine whether your experience and expression of anger were sinful or righteous.

10. Using the definition given in this chapter, think through your current and past relationships and determine if any of them are characterized by a lack of forgiveness. If they are, get the process started so freedom returns to that relationship.

Chapter 2—Charting a Course: Exploring Your Anger

1. Our image for exploring anger has been the early pilgrims arriving on the east coast of North America. Seriously examining the interior of our lives is not an easy task. Tune in to your own experience of exploring anger. What images come to mind? What feelings are you experiencing as you embark on this adventure? What are your fears and anxieties?

2. Sometimes we find out about ourselves by observing others. As you read about the various people at Mountainview Bible Church, who do you identify with the most? In what ways are your experiences and expression of anger the same? In what ways are they different?

3. Go back to those people again and make some assumptions. What kinds of experiences do you think existed in their respective histories? Did they externalize or internalize their anger? Did their strategy work for them? The goal here is to get in touch with the rich variety we experience as we explore our anger and that of others.

4. We have suggested that pride and humility play a major role in how we deal with our own histories and preferences. It is natural for us to adopt the moral high ground on our own viewpoints and assume everything and everyone else is defi-

cient. Can you think of an area in your life where this perspective on pride and humility makes sense?

5. Think of an illustration of anger in the Bible. Take our "Person (P) + Experience (E) = Outcome (O)" equation and analyze the biblical story through this grid. Seek as much detail and specificity as possible.

6. Jackie thought that Joe's experience of anger was irrational and absurd. Think of a recent situation where you had that reaction to someone else's anger. If you know them well, have a conversation that will help you understand the experiences and expectations that precipitated their response.

7. We would suggest that you explore the fruit on your family tree, especially with respect to anger expression. It takes courage. Be sure to clarify in your mind that in exploring one's family of origin the purpose is not to attribute intention or to assign guilt to any family member. To do either of those things engenders a sense of disloyalty and guilt, which destroys the freedom we need to explore the behavior patterns. Work hard to focus on the behavior manifested and your response to it, not the intention of the other persons. In fact, it is helpful to intentionally attribute acceptable intention or motivation to others while focusing on the behavior and our response to it.

Here is the plan. Look at each family member—father, mother, siblings, and self. How was anger expressed by each? Write it down, making brief notes. When you have completed that task, move to the question of how each responded when anger was expressed by other family members. You have noted the differences in expression; now focus on the differences in response to anger expressed by others. You could be creative and set this up in a chart form. Get as clear a picture as you can. Feel free to consult carefully with others in your family or others who have had opportunity to observe your family. You are doing a nonjudgmental analysis of anger experience and expression in your family of origin. Don't get too serious; we are exploring with tentativeness, not judgment. When we discover something that facilitates our learning, we will know it. We are opening ourselves to explore, with appropriate caution, territory we may not have entered before so let's not jump too quickly to premature conclusions about what we see. Sharing these explorations with your pastoral counselor will help as we seek learning that will facilitate our growth.

8. Is your expression of anger more frequently imploding or exploding? Are you aware of feelings, thoughts, or actions that are directed toward yourself? Or, are you more aware of anger exploding outward toward others, God, or things? Keep a diary of your anger for a few weeks. Simply acknowledge, accept, and catalogue your experiences. In writing the diary your purpose is not to analyze each entry, but to accumulate a sufficient number of entries. When you have ten or twelve accounts, then you may reflect on them. Study to see if imploding or exploding was more common. Do you see any patterns?

9. Masks do not just hide us from others, but also keep us out of touch with ourselves. We have talked about masks of implosion, physiology, verbal behavior, and other behaviors. Can you identify your major masks? Are there some you would like to gently remove? Are there some that others might help you identify more carefully?

10. At the end of this chapter we have provided an illustration of nonproductive and productive anger cycles. Pull out a few of your recent anger episodes and try and work them through the cycle, seeking to determine whether they were productive or nonproductive and why.

Chapter 3—The Power of Feelings: Sin or Righteousness?

1. Many of us spend time in small group meetings, like the deacons group under discussion in this chapter. It may be in the context of church, work, a social club, a community group, or whatever. Think back to a recent example of con-

flict in your group. Are there "Garths" in your group? "Doreens"? "Michaels"? Where do you fit, in terms of the way you handle anger in a meeting?

2. Garth and Doreen were able to gain insight when some time had passed after the meeting. Some people are like that by disposition. They do not fully understand what is going on around them or inside them at the time, but they can process it more accurately later. The key is that these people need to give themselves both permission and a space to do that. Are you like that? Do you intentionally allow yourself the freedom to do the processing after a meeting where there has been conflict?

3. Do you have a spouse, friend, or roommate that could function like Dorothy functioned with Garth? Can you ask them explicitly to help you talk through a difficult situation so your insight is deepened? Often our best self-understanding is cultivated in community.

4. Keep a journal of times when you are angry in the next week. Simply write down the feeling and the situation in which it occurred. When the week is over, go back to each situation and ask the why question: Why did I get angry in that situation? See how many incidents force you to look in at thwarted goals, values, expectations, or self-worth and how many put you into the blame game where you are holding someone else responsible. Make some decisions about how you would like to live in this particular area.

5. Garth became aware that his battered personal worth had played a major role in his display of anger. All of us have had difficult experiences in life where our personal worth becomes threatened, damaged, or bruised. How would you assess your sense of personal worth at the present time? Is any work needed in this sphere of life? Are you seeing any indications that you are responding to feedback or constructive criticism with defensiveness and fear?

6. The next time you are angry with someone for what they did or said or did not do or did not say, work through the Person (P) material that you brought to the event and then sit down with them and talk through it. Often in social inter-

action we are able to clarify some of our own baggage, and we also are letting the person know that they are not completely to blame for what went on.

7. Take out some paper and complete the following sentences: Feelings. . . . ; God thinks that feelings. . . . ; My family taught me that feelings. . . . ; When I see people show their feelings I. . . . ; When I think of feelings, I wish. . . . Answer honestly and openly by writing down the first thing that comes into your mind. When you have finished, do not reread it. A week later come back to what you have written and see what it tells you about yourself. What areas need work? How does your history with feelings affect the way you are at present?

8. Take the threefold distinction between acknowledge, accept, and approve and use it to analyze various feelings, including anger. Do you work through all these stages or are you a person who quickly jumps to the conclusion "I should not be feeling that" before you have fully acknowledged and accepted that you are feeling it?

9. Read through the Gospels (Matthew, Mark, Luke, and John) and make a note of every passage that comments on or alludes to self-righteousness. Commit a few of the key passages to memory and pray that you will keep this mask out of your life.

10. In evangelical circles you will hear the phrase "righteous indignation" used when the topic of anger comes up. Unfortunately, this is a noncommunicative phrase in that everyone will have different criteria for the nature of "righteous" and "indignation." It is much more helpful to speak of some of the words used in Scripture. For example, *thumos* and *orge* provide us with three viewpoints on anger. In all cases, the fits of rage described in the first word are wrong. In the second word, we can be angry with or without a spirit of personal animosity and vengeance lurking behind it. Ask the Lord to give you clarity on the difference between these three and use them as a grid or paradigm to bring to the world of anger.

Chapter 4—Triggers and Thoughts: Thinking Effectively about Your Anger

1. Garth made a decision to do his self-exploration in the context of community; that is, he decided to seek out the help of his pastor to provide insight and perspective. Outside help can be personal from a friend, pastoral from someone in that role, or professional from a trained counselor. As you reflect on your own anger issues, list a couple of people who might fit into each of these categories. Are you at a stage where you would benefit from some outside help?

2. Given the link of anger with the body, do an inventory on yourself. The next time you are angry, tune in to your body. What are you feeling? Where are you feeling it? What kinds of sensations are going through your body? Do you get sick or have unusual aches or pains when you are intensely angry? This level of self-awareness can often make us more conscious of when we are angry and why.

3. We have talked about rifles and fuses to illustrate triggers. Can you think of other images or symbols that represent triggers? How do these images help you understand your own anger?

4. Let us suggest that you explore your triggers. One way to do this is to explore your feelings at the triggering point in the equation of anger. Find an analogy, a picture of how you felt at that point. Would the word "blocked," "frustrated," "steamed," "exasperated," "put down," "overlooked," "run over," "stabbed," or "forgotten" best describe your sensation at that point? You add your words. Creating imagery that captures and pictures your feelings or thoughts related to the triggering of anger is very helpful. The imagery you create may enable self-exploration.

5. We have provided brief biographical sketches of Garth, Doreen, and Sally. Do a brief sketch of yourself by noting a few key incidents that you think have produced triggers. This is not a form of a "blame game" in that we are trying to get you to dump on your past. It is more for the benefit

of fresh understanding so that you can take full responsibility for your reactions.

6. Read the fourth chapter of Jonah carefully. Picture what happened in your mind. Obviously, the chapter does not outline all the details, but see if you can fill some in. What do you think Jonah was going through? What was he feeling? What kinds of physiological responses were present? Can you put some specific sentences under Jonah's goals, values, expectations, and personal worth? What was God going through as he listened to Jonah? Explore this entire story in some depth and detail.

7. Philippians 2:5 is an extremely important verse to understand. What does it mean to you? How can you put it into practice specifically? Do a study of the verse by linking other relevant passages with it.

8. "Pride" and "humility" are two of those words that we hear and think we understand but there is a lot more to them than we realize. Take two sheets of paper. At the top of one of them write: Times When I Am Humble; at the top of the other: Times When I Am Proud. Obviously, the first sheet runs some risks, but you are not bragging about your humility—just trying to understand how it shows itself in your life! Do you have any examples that tie into any of our discussions on these topics?

9. The next time you are angry at something or someone, write one sentence down beside goal, value, expectation, and personal worth. Write specific and succinct sentences that capture the thinking process you were going through at the time of anger. Then write four other sentences that would not have produced anger. Make some decisions to clarify your commitments before you hit particular circumstances.

10. As people respond toward you, become conscious of the distinction between behavior and intention. On the one hand, this is what they are doing. On the other, this is what they intend. Watch and see whether you attribute intent to others' behavior and what happens to you when you do. In close relationships, watch the natural tendency to get into conflict over what was meant, rather than what was done.

Chapter 5—Avoiding Vengeance: Behaving Righteously

1. The "sharing concerns" syndrome is rampant in many evangelical churches. Do you find yourself "sharing concerns" in a hostile way? Is there a more accurate way to describe what you are doing? Have you ever been on the receiving end of this? What did it feel like?

2. The next time you confront someone or are confronted by someone, separate the content from the style. Often problems are created because of the way we confront, not because of the content. As you reflect on the Bert–Salvatore interaction, list a number of stylistic alternatives that could have been utilized to make this a more productive exchange for both parties.

3. Commit the words of Romans 12:17–21 to memory. This is a wonderful passage to bring to communal life and the messiness of relationships.

4. List some relationships where you have tried everything to bring resolution and found that you were unsuccessful. What feelings does that produce in you? Do you feel regret? remorse? guilt? discomfort? a lack of resolution? How do the words of Romans 12:18 impact these situations?

5. The biblical notion of love is behaviorally oriented. Our contemporary culture has moved love into the realm of the emotive. Reflect on this difference and write down the practical implications of this. For example, for those of us who are married, loving your spouse will be understood in very different ways, depending on the definition we bring to the word "love."

6. Take a concordance or word study book and trace the teaching about forgiveness in the Bible. Focus on both the vertical and horizontal components of it. List some of the specific behaviors that forgiveness requires and demands. How might these show themselves in your everyday life?

7. Luke 17 puts the responsibility for forgiveness with the offended rather than with the offender. In some sense this

flies in the face of our sense of justice. Think of a relation-ship where you have really had to work at forgiveness. Has the other person responded in ways that you have found facilitating? Have you felt a lack of response from them? How can the words of Luke 17 inform this relationship so you both experience more freedom?

8. Because of some inaccurate teaching on anger, some Christians believe that the passive communication style is the best one. Why do you think this might be? Is there any part of biblical theology that would lead us to be negating what we believe and think?

9. Do you know any aggressive people? What does it feel like to be on the receiving end of their bulldozing? What do you feel about yourself when they act this way? Can you level with any of them and let them know how you feel?

10. We have suggested that assertiveness affirms freedom, worth, and community. List some of the qualities or characteristics involved in assertive responses. Can you work on any of these as a way of expressing your anger behaviorally?

ENDNOTES

i. *Thumos* and other derivations of the word can be found twenty times in the New Testament (Matt. 2:16; Luke 4:28; Acts 12:20; 19:28; Rom. 2:8; 2 Cor. 12:20; Gal. 5:20; Eph. 4:31; Col. 3:8; Heb. 11:27; Rev. 12:12; 14:8, 10, 19; 15:1, 7; 16:1, 19; 18:3; 19:15).

ii. *Parorgismos* and other derivations of the word can be found three times in the New Testament (Rom. 10:19; Eph. 4:26; 6:4).

iii. *Orge* and other derivations of the word can be found forty-two times in the New Testament (Matt. 3:7; 5:22; 18:34; 22:7; Mark 3:5; Luke 3:7; 14:21; 15:28; 21:23; John 3:36; Rom. 1:18; 2:5, 8; 3:5; 4:15; 5:9; 9:22; 12:19; 13:4–5; Eph. 2:3; 4:26, 31; 5:6; Col. 3:6, 8; 1 Thess. 1:10; 2:16; 5:9; 1 Tim. 2:8; Titus 1:7; Heb. 3:11; 4:3; James 1:19–20; Rev. 6:16–17; 11:18; 12:17; 14:10; 16:19; 19:15).

iv. *Aganaktesis* and other derivations of the word can be found eight times in the New Testament (Matt. 20:24; 21:15; 26:8; Mark 10:14, 41; 14:4; Luke 13:14; 2 Cor. 7:11).

REFERENCES

Adams, J. E. *Competent to Counsel.* Nutley, N.J.: Presbyterian and Reformed, 1970.

Augsburger, D. W. *Anger and Assertiveness in Pastoral Care.* Philadelphia: Fortress, 1979.

———. *The Freedom of Forgiveness.* Chicago: Moody, 1984.

Benner, D. *Strategic Pastoral Counseling.* Grand Rapids: Baker, 1992.

Berkowitz, L. Experimental investigations of hostility catharsis. *Journal of Consulting and Clinical Psychology* 35:1–7, 1970.

Brand, P,. and P. Yancey. *Pain: The Gift Nobody Wants.* New York: HarperCollins, 1993.

Kassinove, H. (ed.) *Anger Disorders.* Washington: Taylor and Francis, 1995.

Knowles, M. *The Adult Learner.* Houston: Gulf, 1973.

Lerner, H. G. *The Dance of Anger.* New York: Harper and Row, 1985.

Lewis, W. A., and A. M. Bucher. Anger, catharsis, the reformulated frustration—aggression hypothesis, and health consequences. *Psychotherapy* 29:385–92, 1992.

Myers, D. *Journal of Psychology and Christianity,* September 1996. *At time of submission this article was misplaced!

Nouwen, H. J. *Reaching Out.* New York: Doubleday, 1975.

Potter-Efron, R. and P. *Anger, Alcoholism and Addiction.* New York: Norton, 1991.

Rogers, C. 1969. *Book misplaced at time of submission.

Simon, S. B. and S. *Forgiveness.* New York: Warner, 1990.

Warren, R., and R. T. Kurlychek. Treatment of maladaptive anger and aggression: Catharsis vs. behavior therapy. *Corrective and Social Psychiatry and Journal of Behavior Technology* 27:135–39, 1981.

Waters, D. B., and E. C. Lawrence. *Competence, Courage and Change.* New York: Norton, 1991.

Watkins, C. E. The effects of counselor self-disclosure: A research review. *The Counseling Psychologist* 18:477–500, 1990.

Wilson, R. *Counseling and Community.* Dallas: Word, 1995.

ANNOTATED BIBLIOGRAPHY

Adams, J. E. *Competent to Counsel*. Nutley, N.J.: Presbyterian and Reformed, 1970. Adams's first major treatise on the importance of nouthetic counseling.

Augsburger, D. W. *Anger and Assertiveness in Pastoral Care*. Philadelphia: Fortress, 1979. Examines ways to channel anger with constructive communication strategies.

———. *The Freedom of Forgiveness*. Chicago: Moody, 1984. A simple book that outlines the freedom that the Christian experiences when they are willing to pay the price of forgiveness.

Bassett, R. L. et al. Righteous and sinful anger from the perspectives of Christian therapists and college students. *Journal of Psychology and Christianity* 8:47–56, 1989. An experimental study utilizing Christian therapists that seeks to examine the relationship between righteous and sinful anger.

Brand, P., and P. Yancey. *Pain: The Gift Nobody Wants*. New York: HarperCollins, 1993. An excellent discussion of pain with insights transferable to emotional pain.

Carlson, D. L. *Overcoming Hurts and Anger*. Eugene, Oreg.: Harvest House, 1981. Deals broadly with negative emotions providing some good biblical understanding and helpful ways to think about anger.

Dryden, W. *Dealing with Anger Problems*. Sarasota, Fla.: Professional Resource Exchange, 1990. Presents a rational-emotive approach to anger in the form of a guidebook that provides counselors with specific interventions.

Fein, M. L. *Integrated Anger Management*. Westport, Conn.: Praeger, 1993. Discusses the positive aspects of anger and the way to utilize it in social situations.

Gaultiere, W. J. A biblical perspective on therapeutic treatment of client anger at God. *Journal of Psychology and Christianity* 8:38–46, 1989. Using the examples of Job and the psalmist, this article examines ways to help people resolve their anger at God.

Hargrave, T. D. *Families and Forgiveness*. New York: Brunner/Mazel, 1994. Describes therapeutic process to move clients from insight, understanding, and compensation through to forgiveness in the context of their families.

Kassinove, H. (ed.) *Anger Disorders*. Washington: Taylor and Francis, 1995. More clinical book that reviews theories of anger and focuses on anger disorders that are disruptive.

Knowles, M. *The Adult Learner*. Houston: Gulf, 1973. A classic text on an area that is important in the process of Strategic Pastoral Counseling.

Lerner, H. G. *The Dance of Anger*. New York: Harper and Row, 1985. Although the primary focus of this book is anger and women, it is a helpful tool for understanding anger in all relationships.

Lewis, C. S. *God in the Dock: Essays on Theology and Ethics.* Grand Rapids: Eerdmans, 1970. Contains one of Lewis's famous essays on the modern approach to God that puts humanity in the role of judge and God in the courtroom dock.

Myers, D. *Journal of Psychology and Christianity,* September 1996. *At time of submission this article was misplaced!

Nouwen, H. J. *Reaching Out.* New York: Doubleday, 1975. Nouwen's work is a rich resource. It is his articulation of hospitality that will be a useful way for counselors to think of their relationship to counselees.

Oliver, G. J., and H. N. Wright. *When Anger Hits Home.* Chicago: Moody, 1992. A helpful discussion of anger in the family and of the myths and the gift of anger.

Peterson, E. *The Message.* Colorado Springs: NavPress, 1993. A refreshing version of the New Testament in contemporary English. Makes old truths refreshingly new, particularly in areas like anger.

Potter-Efron, R. and P. *Anger, Alcoholism and Addiction.* New York: Norton, 1991. Integrates theoretical and practical aspects of anger with addictions and provides clinicians with treatment strategies.

———. *Letting Go of Anger.* Oakland: New Harbinger, 1995. Focuses on styles of anger by providing readers with self-tests.

Rainey, S. B. *Anger.* Colorado Springs: NavPress, 1992. Discussion guide style of book that approaches anger in the Institute of Biblical Counseling (Larry Crabb) framework.

Rogers, C. *Book misplaced at time of submission.

Simon, S. B. and S. *Forgiveness.* New York: Warner, 1990. Practical book that teaches forgiveness is a sign of emotional strength and is the antidote to making peace with our past.

Smedes, L. B. *Forgive and Forget.* New York: Harper and Row, 1984. Guides the reader through four major steps toward forgiveness—hurting, hating, healing, and reconciliation.

Stoop, D., and S. Arterburn. *The Angry Man.* Vancouver: Word, 1991. This book helps us to see the origins of anger and to move toward healing in new ways to relate.

Swindoll, C. R. *Laugh Again.* Vancouver: Word, 1992. In his inimitable way, Swindoll expounds the Philippian epistle with helpful insight and application.

Warren, N. C. *Make Anger Your Ally.* Colorado Springs: Focus on the Family, 1990. Helpful in understanding the physiology of anger with many illustrations that help one to visualize success in dealing with anger.

Waters, D. B., and E. C. Lawrence. *Competence, Courage and Change.* New York: Norton, 1991. This book offers an alternative to a pathological approach to counseling by focusing on the healthy urges. It identifies the strengths and resources that people bring to their lives and encourages us to build on these to develop new strategies for coping.

Wilson, R. *Counseling and Community.* Dallas: Word, 1995. Examines the relationship between the world of the private counselor and the local church, arguing that a greater commitment to a communal sensibility is needed in counseling.